the
longview

Lasting Strategies for Rising Leaders

Roger Parrott, PhD

David C Cook

transforming lives together

To MaryLou, Grady, and Madison

THE LONGVIEW
Published by David C. Cook
4050 Lee Vance View
Colorado Springs, CO 80918 U.S.A.

David C. Cook Distribution Canada
55 Woodslee Avenue, Paris, Ontario, Canada N3L 3E5

David C. Cook U.K., Kingsway Communications
Eastbourne, East Sussex BN23 6NT, England

Unless otherwise indicated, all Scripture quotations are taken from the
New Living Translation of the Holy Bible. New Living Translation
copyright © 1996, 2004 by Tyndale Charitable Trust. Used by
permission of Tyndale House Publishers. All rights reserved.

LCCN 2009932540
ISBN 978-1-4347-6749-3
eISBN 978-1-4347-0067-4

Published in association with the Eames Literary Services, LLC, Nashville, TN.

The Team: Don Pape, Brian Thomasson, Caitlyn York, Karen Athen
Cover Design: Amy Kiechlin

Printed in Canada
First Edition 2009

1 2 3 4 5 6 7 8 9 10

072309

Contents

Acknowledgments

I have been blessed with a group of people whom God strategically placed in my life in order to get the ideas of *The Longview* onto paper.

MaryLou—Nothing I do matters without you, and all that matters to me revolves around you. You are God's most generous gift for leadership in my life.

Grady and Madison—The patience you showed through the months of Dad writing this book is just the tip of the iceberg of your love, maturity, and quality. I'm proud of you for who you are, not what you do—whether that be as a leader, a follower, or a get-out-of-the-wayer.

Brian Thomasson—Your insights as an editor went far beyond anything I ever expected. I am forever grateful for your wisdom in gathering the big picture, wrestling with the ideas, and communicating it all with precision. You're a remarkable rising younger leader I want to follow.

Belhaven Board of Trustees—I cherish the privilege to team with you as we consider soaring ideas and tackle difficult challenges. For your unwavering support through the years I'm deeply grateful. And for your insistence that I set aside time to write this book—and even adding it to my annual review—I'm most appreciative.

Charles Cannada—I cannot imagine there is a better board chair among all ministries and colleges. I appreciate the godly and practical wisdom you apply to the tough issues, the energy with which you analyze and champion opportunities, and your amazing ability to always take the longview.

Les Parrott—You're a brother in this journey, a brother in the Lord, and my younger brother of whom I'm really proud. Thanks for being such a help and encouragement through this process.

Marcia Carroll was organized enough to keep this project going with all else I do in the office. Susan Springer and the Belhaven College librarians are the best researchers in the business. Richard Felix challenged me to write and wouldn't take excuses.

John Eames has been a wonderful guide through the maze of the literary world. Caitlyn York made the tough revisions to assure this work was stronger and clearer. Ingrid Beck got us to the target on time. Don Pape was willing to make this project a priority. Thanks!

Along with these who enabled *The Longview* to go from ideas to a finished book, I am thankful for a host of special leadership mentors the Lord has brought to me at critical phases of life (in chronological order):

Leslie Parrott, my father, was a practically perfect leader in every way. I miss you, Dad. And to my mother, Lora Lee, I owe the invaluable habit of applying fortitude and optimism to overcome every leadership challenge.

Lee McCleery stretched me early on in the pastorate and championed me when I was too young to know better.

Roger Kelsey was a doctoral advisor who saw leadership in me long before I recognized it.

Curt Smith took a huge risk on a young college administrator and gave to me much more responsibility than I had earned. His wife, Marg, was my strongest advocate and a remarkable leader in her own right. For MaryLou and me, Curt and Marg shaped our leadership journey more than anyone else.

Leighton Ford opened the broader evangelical world to me and modeled the deeper spiritual qualities of leadership.

Tom Zimmerman showed me a whole different level of effective administrative leadership and tacked down every corner just right.

Paul Cedar taught me to practice godly patience by listening for what the Lord is saying, and it has been a joy to partner with him in the walk of leadership around the world.

The Belhaven College vice presidents are all first-class leaders with whom I am privileged to work daily. I find in our iron-sharpening-iron relationship a continual opportunity to learn.

This book represents a lifetime of experience, work, successes, and mistakes that were all blended in my life through continual learning from insightful mentors, timely training, and the joys as well as the bumps and bruises of leadership. God has been gracious to allow my life to intersect with so many wonderful people and to see up close the remarkable workings of the Lord in my own shop and all around the world.

To Jesus I owe everything.

The Challenge: Take the Longview

We live in a quick-fix, immediate-impact, short-view world.

But we serve a longview God.

To bridge this gulf between earthly priorities and a heavenly perspective, Jesus became the ultimate example of longview leadership amid the clamor for expedient results. Of course His sights were always aimed toward eternity (the ultimate longview), and He lived and thought in that realm. But even in the practical everyday demands of leadership, Jesus showed us the value of investing in longview solutions as we serve those in our care.

Matthew records for us a string of events that could have come out quite differently had it not been for Jesus' willingness to take a longview approach to a mundane administrative demand.

After hearing that Herod had beheaded John the Baptist, Jesus went alone to the mountains to grieve. But crowds followed Him to the remote area where He had gone, and soon He was pulled from His isolation to heal the sick and teach. As evening came, His disciples, who wanted to help solve a brewing challenge, told Him, "This is a remote place, and it's already getting late. Send the crowds away so they can go to the villages and buy food for themselves" (Matt. 14:15). The committee's decision seemed like a reasonable solution in these circumstances, and it would have been an easy fix for Jesus as He dealt with His grief.

But Jesus took a longview perspective in mentoring these disciples, knowing the solution had sweeping ramifications beyond where to get dinner. He was preparing them for spiritual growth to come by including them in feeding the multitude with just a few pieces of bread and two fish. As usual, it was far more than the immediate problem alone that Jesus was addressing—although that in itself would have been enough.

Instead, bolstered by the miracle on the hillside, Peter found the faith that very evening to step out of the boat and walk on water. In the following weeks, a faith-filled Peter spoke for the group when he declared aloud, "You are the Messiah, the Son of the living God" (Matt. 16:16). And just a few days after that bold profession, Peter was invited to climb another mountain—this time to bear witness to Jesus in His transfigured fullness talking with Moses and Elijah as the bright cloud of God came over them all.

After the feeding of the five thousand, we see the disciples, and especially Peter, becoming true men of faith with whom Jesus could leave the earthly leadership of His church. Their spiritual climb, it can be argued, started with Jesus taking a longview approach to the demands of day-to-day leadership as dusk was falling on a hillside and hungry people were anxious for a meal. Purposeful action in the routine of leadership is important because those outcomes nearly always have longview implications.

The Longview is written to ministry leaders, but longview principles are for every Christian striving for authentically biblical leadership, whether in ministry or the marketplace. How will you choose to face the challenges of leadership? Will you choose to pursue immediate results—or will you choose to follow Christ and have the fortitude, vision, skill, and strength to understand that genuine transformation is gained through envisioning the longview implications of every leadership action?

The Seismic Shift

Longview leadership might have been tenable in past eras when the pace of change was slow, but can it work in a world where careers are built, promotions are offered, and raises are granted on the basis of immediate results? Today's rising leaders have been reared, tutored, and equipped to operate in a world that prizes immediate results. They have inherited a quick-results culture that found its footing in the junk bond and buyout phenomenon of the 1980s. Then came the rapid rise and fall of the dot-coms in the 1990s and the expansion of individual credit-card debt that allowed the immediacy of wants to be valued over long-term needs. Finally, the new millennium brought a real-estate frenzy created by overly leveraged speculators seeking to make fast money by flipping properties they never possessed, and families lulled by subprime financing into buying bigger homes than they could afford with the promise of unrealistic value appreciation.

For three decades skyrocketing incentives have been the norm for all manner of short-term producers—from stockbrokers to college coaches—as leaders at every level have indoctrinated us to believe immediate gains trump long-term consequences. Our expectations for leaders have undergone a seismic shift from longview responsibility to short-view rewards. Summarizing a study that reported 40 percent of CEOs who left their position lasted an average of just 1.8 years, and the average tenure for the lower half of this group was only eight months, *Harvard Business Review* concluded, "Nobody these days gets much time to show what he or she can do."[1] This nearsightedness is eroding the foundational underpinnings of organizational quality and severely handicapping the effectiveness of leaders who are robbing the future to pay for today.

Tragically, even the church has swallowed whole the cultural lie that immediate results are more important than lasting transformation. Our theology and our ministry passion draw us to talk about longview outcomes as our heart's desire, but we have been duped into fostering a generation of leaders, board members, employees, and constituencies who value short-term gain over longview significance. Ministry leaders believe it and act accordingly—hiring and rewarding people who can promote Band-Aid fixes as monumental solutions, creating plans that promise the moon and always come up short, raising funds from unrealistically compressed donor relationships, and touting to boards and constituencies those results that can most easily be measured and applauded.

Because this short-view corporate culture has so permeated the church today, we in ministry have loosened our grip on the biblical model for leadership. We have grown to expect and even demand an ever-increasing cycle of measurable and immediate results from our leaders. Sadly, their careers have become dependent on their weekly and quarterly reports rather than their longview outcomes. Rising ministry leaders have been caught in this ever-tightening vise grip of cultural expectations gone askew.

The Longview Works

The time is right for rising leaders to break free from the short-term leadership patterns of the past and set their sights on the horizon to ensure a life of leadership that will be honoring to God and bring us back to principles that will allow the church to make a transformational difference in the world. The short view doesn't work, but it will continue to permeate our society, direct our actions, and be the gold standard for "success" until purposeful, visionary, and determined leaders pull us back to a longview outlook that seeks lasting value.

As the apostle Paul challenged us in 1 Corinthians 13, it is time to put away childish things and not be wooed by the immediacy of appearing productive by making meaningless sounds like a loud gong or a clanging cymbal. Rather than our noisy quarterly reports, our standard for how we measure success as Christian leaders needs to reflect the longview desires of God, built on values that endure.

As in every aspect of life, God designed the longview as the best path to genuine success and meaningful transformation:

- Balanced eating and exercise always beat fad diets and weight-loss binges for lasting healthy results.

- Relationships grounded in shared core values can last a lifetime, while those based on interest commonalities erode with the seasons.
- Correcting a child through mentoring is always better than only administering punishment, even though behavioral changes may come at an agonizingly slow pace.
- Household budgets built on needs rather than wants survive economic cycles.
- Education that teaches ideas and critical thinking is superior to learning facts, although the first is measured over a lifetime and the second on a pop quiz.
- Working out a Christ-centered worldview—rather than simply proof-texting one's way through the big questions of life—is the only storm-tested framework for living.

If God's pattern is clearly grounded in the longview, why do we continue to seek short-term gains over long-term significance when it comes to leadership?

This contrast between the desire for immediate results and the need for meaningful longview leadership is not new to this generation—although the globalization of information, business, and culture has intensified its effects in the past thirty years. We see this dichotomy playing out at least three thousand years ago in the selection of David as Israel's second king. According to 1 Samuel 16, God sent Samuel, the last of the Hebrew judges, to Bethlehem to select the new king from among Jesse's sons. Samuel looked over the young men and made a judgment based on whom he imagined could most quickly change the volatile leadership situation created by Saul. But God interrupted him and established entirely different criteria for evaluating leadership: "The LORD doesn't see things the way you see them. People judge by outward appearance, but the LORD looks at the heart" (1 Sam. 16:7).

In today's leadership world, our outward appearance is the tally sheet of results we tout to prove our worth, while our thoughts and intentions are buried deep in the longview we bring to leadership.

The Longview Reality Show

Leaders throughout the ages have been drawn to the flashy first impression, the rewards of picking low-hanging fruit, or the approval and support that is garnered from successful fast action. But when a godly longview is our aim, we develop a whole different class of skills, relationships, and priorities that can carry us throughout a lifetime of meaningful leadership, rather than allowing our focus to be fixed solely on the next hurdle ahead.

Ever since television reality shows took over the airwaves, I've imagined a show for leaders. The show puts three leadership teams in a boat race. Of course it is filmed on a beautiful white sandy beach with crystal clear blue water, located in an exotic string of islands in some remote part of the world that makes television producers happy.

Through the weeks, teams compete for the right to select one of three boats available to them: (1) a speedboat that glides over the water at speeds exceeding ninety miles an hour but is vulnerable in rough water; (2) a cabin cruiser designed with strength and stability to handle high seas, although it runs at half the speed of the first boat; and (3) a simple, slow sailboat with a single mast and no mechanical engine.

During each week's episode the contestants are involved in competitions designed to make them look foolish and to drive up ratings. The winners select the boat of their choice to race each week from one small island to the next, building points toward choosing the vessel they prefer for the climactic race for the $1 million prize. The adversaries scheme and plot and humiliate one another, trying to "earn" the right to choose the best boat for the final high-dollar journey.

In the dramatic season finale, each team is set and ready for the race in the boat they have won—the most successful team, betting on good weather, has chosen the high speed of the hydroplane over the strength of the cabin cruiser. Meanwhile the losers of the game (those least effective at sabotaging their competitors) prepare to do their best in the sailboat rejected by the other mariners.

Then, in one of those stunning reality show moments when everything is turned upside down, the tanned and handsome host unveils the finish line for the race—and as they cut to a commercial break, looks of horror and outrage can be seen on the faces of the presumed dominant sailors.

Unlike the previous weeks' races, the finish line is not within the string of islands, but can in fact be reached only by circling the islands multiple times. This is not a distance that can be traveled by either powerboat, for their fuel supply will surely run out long before the race is finished. Only the sailboat, with its ability to catch the wind, has the opportunity to finish the race and win the prize.

Like our imaginary contestants, today's ministry leaders need to learn the value of sailboats over powerboats in completing the race. We are not leaders whose aim should be professional island-hopping; we must equip ourselves for godly circumnavigation. We must return to a proper understanding of the finish line to which God has called us, and internalize the longview way to lead, live, work, and relate to each other. In a longview world, the fastest, flashiest motors we might develop can never outdistance the boat whose sails are filled with God's wind.

Lead as if You'll Be There Forever

The heart of the longview does not begin with actions as much as attitude. Imagine that the organization and position you are in right now is what God wants you to do for the rest of your professional life. For many, it might be discouraging to truly feel "locked in" to your job. But contrary to the mantras of popular career gurus, this is one of the best things that could ever happen to you and your ministry, because only from that immobile position will your outlook on leadership be revolutionized.

To live without professional advancement opportunities would, of course, be demotivating and create an unhealthy situation for both you and your ministry. But to lead as if you must remain in that same position forever—and live with the long-term consequences of every decision—will shift your perspective, align your priorities, and build lasting strength in your organization, rather than allowing you to settle for the comfort and accolades of immediate results.

When a leader is thinking, living, and acting in terms of only the short range, everyone around him suffers and may be handicapped for years to come because the decisions of today will narrow subsequent options and opportunities. The compounding weight of each shortsighted decision speeds the deterioration of the ministry's foundation, while a long-term perspective strengthens that substructure for a higher reach in the future.

Longview Decision Making

When President Jimmy Carter held a thirteen-day summit at Camp David in 1978 with Egyptian president Anwar el Sadat and Israeli prime minister Menachem Begin, a formal state of war still existed between the two countries, with Egypt determined to reclaim the Sinai territory seized by the Israelis twenty-two years previously. In the woods of Maryland, these long-hoped-for negotiations came to multiple stalemates. But each time Carter found a way to keep the discussion alive, even though deep-seated mistrust between the two Middle Eastern leaders kept them from talking directly to each other, causing the U. S. president to shuttle between their private cabins, triangulating the dialogue.

On the morning of the eleventh day, the arduous process appeared to disintegrate when Prime Minister Begin decided to leave the meetings over the wording of a side letter on the status of Jerusalem. He wouldn't have his mind changed by the immediate needs of securing the peace in the Middle East and freeing his country from the relentless cycle of violence. But with brilliant insight, President Carter shifted the perspective from the immediate results to the long-term implications: as Prime Minister Begin was packing his bags to leave, President Carter brought to him eight personalized, autographed pictures of the three leaders working together, and told the prime minister they were for him to take home to his eight grandchildren so they would always remember what the three men had tried to accomplish together. With a new long-term perspective, Begin unpacked and days later signed the Camp David Accords.

Now, while it is certainly true that a decision regarding what is best for the immediate may often be the same as the choice that is best for the future, it is essential that leaders get into the groove of thinking beyond the near horizon. Otherwise, they lose the proper perspective that allows them to consider long-term issues and ramifications.

When short-term triumphs take precedence over long-term success, those same aggressive leadership skills can deteriorate into selfish decisions, fearful management, and self-deceiving evaluation. And the longer a leader continues in this pattern, the more troublesome the consequences and limiting the solution options. Eventually, a leader can become entrapped in a cycle that demands ignoring the mounting crisis of the future in order to sustain the appearance of current success.

The Short Run Never Works for Long

Here is a vivid way to grasp the problem that short-term perspective brings into your ministry. Think back to that time when you had a great employee who, because of family or career issues, began to seek a new position. The search was not far enough along for you to be brought into the discussion, but mentally the employee had already moved on—and you knew it.

Even if the job-searching employee was one of your key players, that individual had already been demoted, in your view, from the person around whom you were building a future to one whose contribution was suspect at best.

In that rapid transformation, the only attribute that had changed about the employee was his perspective. He still came to work with the same skill set, same hours, same types of ideas, and same energy. But because his viewpoint was now focused only on the short run, you could not count on him to make decisions that were in the long-term best interest of the ministry. Now multiply that scenario into the life of a CEO or other top leader—not just a rising employee—and consider the potential damage.

A short-term leadership perspective is devastating in ministry, but the impact can be illustrated best in the corporate world, where results are totaled on the bottom line. Recently, Japanese automaker Toyota did what the captains of industry once considered impossible—it surpassed the century-long domination of General Motors as the leading automaker. Could it be that a major factor in the growth of Toyota, Nissan, Honda, Mazda, Subaru, and Mitsubishi is that Japanese leadership expected they would remain with the same company for a lifetime? Fifty years ago Toyota's board and top management implemented a comprehensive plan to accomplish what is being realized today. In contrast, GM's leadership remained primarily focused on their latest quarterly earnings projections during those same years.

The best leaders understand they should always be held accountable for the long term before they are rewarded for their immediate results. The pastor who envisions reaching his whole city will always be more effective than the one who is concerned about making a glowing report at the next conference gathering. A fund-raising professional who desires to build relationships matching donors with their passions will always raise more money than one striving to meet an urgent campaign goal. Over time, even the school administrator who fixes the nagging plumbing problem will be appreciated more than the one who spends that same money to install new carpeting.

The *Harvard Business Review* analysis "If Brands Are Built over Years, Why Are They Managed over Quarters?" explored why short-term thinking dominates business marketing today even though branding is an extremely long-term process. The researchers determined that companies have shifted their focus to quarterly outcomes over long-term success because of three factors. First, there is an abundance of real-time immediate data that allows corporate leaders to measure results in great detail in ways we could not in the past. Second, at the same time, long-term results have become even more difficult to measure, thus pushing the focus to a short-run agenda. And third, the tenure of managers is continually becoming shorter as they see their future linked to demonstrating immediate results.[1]

Endemic Nearsightedness

It is critical to understand that the root of this pattern does not rest only at the feet of self-serving or shortsighted leaders, because boards and constituencies have allowed organizational success to become measured by quarterly results rather than long-term success.

The most public firings of CEOs seem to nearly always reflect a pattern of cheers for that leader through a relatively short period of repeated quarterly reports and then a startling discovery by the board of serious foundational issues gone awry. But these same boards have demanded, rewarded, and praised immediate success at all costs. The real irony is that these boards have also learned to solve their crisis with a short-term solution of firing the CEO, rather than doing the hard work needed to correct the foundational issues—and the cycle is likely to repeat down the road.

And then there are the what-have-you-done-for-me-lately employees or constituents that press leaders for decisions that feed the hunger of instant gratification instead of long-term results. From outside the corner office, pressure has mounted for leaders to make decisions only in light of short-run objectives if those choices will boost today's benefits. But in reality, the foundational erosion caused by decisions guided only by short-term vision will eventually undermine or destroy all the good that has been achieved, because the damage will eventually be discovered and will be difficult and costly to repair.

This same pattern holds true in ministry: We have become focused on measuring the short-term results of our work; e.g., the proposals we write to foundations promise immediate outcomes.

The transformation of lives for the long term is only measured in eternity, and thus it is nearly impossible for us to track the impact of our most significant work.

Boards and CEOs want to hire people who have demonstrated measurable results. But when we overvalue the short-term results that are more easily measured, we in turn reward leaders who produce immediate advances over long-term ministry significance.

Accordingly, the most "productive" people are always being tempted to move to a new place of service.

Instead, the commitment to lead with a longview will transform how you approach leadership more so than any other shift you could make. No matter what your tenure horizon may be—whether you are just starting a new job, considering a change, or fast approaching retirement—if you make decisions as if you will remain in your current position forever, you'll make dramatically better choices and make them for the right reasons.

Fast Wins Eventually Lose

One of my especially fun projects was starting a football team at Belhaven College several years ago, and building on our successful model, I had a number of college-president friends also launch football programs. One of my peers, who wanted to get started right at his university, hired a coaching staff who were strong Christians, well known in the football world, and wonderfully experienced—they knew their Xs and Os. They recruited talented players, created an intense football atmosphere for the team, generated lots of press coverage, and won football games. What the president didn't realize at the time was his coaches were focused on gaining attention-grabbing success in order to move on to the big leagues of coaching.

The university discovered over time that the scholarships were overspent, the dropout rate among players was astronomical, and many of the recruited athletes did not care about the benchmarks of character that were important in attracting students to a Christian school. The president finally overturned a rock exposing how bad it had become when a conference official told him about a horrible intrasquad brawl the coaches were trying to keep under wraps. His "go-to" coaches became his "be-gone" coaches in a hurry, and the school spent several years sweeping up the mess to build integrity into the program, balance out the money, and quiet the sports bloggers. Interestingly, none of those coaches ever made it in Division I football.

The consequences of not making decisions as if you'll be there forever will create an unseen and quietly eroding process that always has the same predictable outcome—it is expensive and time consuming to fix. The harm created by near-focused leaders may be imperceptible at first and the impact may not be seen for years or sometimes decades to come—but the problems created when leaders are not guarding the long-term future will be complex to solve and will limit the opportunities for sustained success.

What's Your View?

To protect against this crippling pattern, a bit of periodic self-evaluation will reveal your current longitudinal view in leadership responsibilities:

- If you knew you could *never* have a different job, which decisions over the past year might you have made differently?
- Do you find yourself putting off a difficult personnel issue or a hard decision in hopes that someone else in the future will have to deal with it instead?

- Which of your recent decisions made you feel most proud? Were they made in light of the long-term implications or the short-term impact?
- Have you purposefully made decisions recently that were best for the long run, even though another choice would have made you look good in the short term?
- What will your legacy with your ministry look like twenty-five years after you are gone?

As you attempt to answer these questions yourself, consider that every leader's responsibility is to fulfill a calling rather than gratify immediate desires. Jesus taught us the ultimate example of never wavering from a long-term view when we have been called to a purpose.

In the garden of Gethsemane He prayed, "My soul is crushed with grief to the point of death.... If it is possible, let this cup of suffering be taken away from me" (Matt. 26:38–39). Although fully God, Jesus was also fully man, and that is the cry of an anguished leader at the crossroads, one longing to give in to the short-term options rather than the long-term objective. Had Jesus taken the immediate view and revealed His power, the mockers would have been silenced, His followers' political dreams would have been accomplished, and the whole world would have been left amazed. But instead, He made a decision from the perspective of forever and prayed, "Father! If this cup cannot be taken away unless I drink it, your will be done" (Matt. 26:42). And like Jesus, a Christian leader's proper long-range view must extend all the way into eternity.

Eternal Results

During the modern missions movement God built His church through people who committed themselves to a long-term outlook.

William Carey, the first missionary to India, worked for seven years before he had his first convert.

Robert Morrison, the first Protestant missionary to China, labored for a quarter century and had fewer than a dozen converts.

The missionaries to East Africa in the early 1800s shipped their goods to their new home in coffins because they didn't expect to return any other way.

These leaders, and thousands whose stories are not remembered, valued the longview significance of ministry over short-run measurable "success." By tilling the soil for future returns, their results are recorded in eternity.

In an age of mobility and global connectedness, God is not likely to call you to only one place of service during your career. But no matter where He calls you, you need to think, work, live, and commit as if it is the only future God has entrusted to you.

Becoming a college president at age thirty-four, I didn't assume my first school in rural Kansas would be my last. But to assure I was always protecting the long-term interests of the institution, I met regularly with a group I privately called "those who will be buried in the local cemetery." I wanted to be sure that the perspectives of the long-term faculty, who would be part of the school long after I left, were always considered when I made decisions.

The day a leader begins to look at his or her responsibility in terms of a limited future is the day leadership effectiveness begins to spiral downward. And while leaders who base decisions on a long-term perspective may not be as flashy in their immediate results, they hire better people, build foundations of constituency strength, preserve organizational infrastructure, and leave a legacy that tells the full story of their success.

2

Deflate Your Ego to Expand Your Influence

The "Dean Scream" is infamous for sinking the presidential bid of the 2004 Democratic early front-runner Howard Dean. At the end of a long Iowa contest, he came into the election night supporters' rally nursing a bad cold that made his voice weak. Bolstered by the enthusiastic crowd, the weary candidate rose to the emotion of the moment to excite them further and finished off his oratory by naming a long list of states where he predicted victory—followed by a final raspy "BYAAAH!" that rang out above the cheers.

Unfortunately for the candidate, the speech was broadcast across the television news syndicates on unidirectional microphones, picking up only his voice and not mixing in the crowd noise around him. Consequently, he sounded as if he were yelling into a battery-operated megaphone that hurt everyone's ears. This distorted reflection of Howard Dean immediately became fodder for late-night talk shows and the 24-7 news cycle, leading to the collapse of the campaign in the following weeks.

It doesn't really matter whether the "Dean scream" was the result of emotion, bad electronics, or the attempt to garner enough energy to overcome the symptoms of a cold. It was heard as a loud, obnoxious megaphone, and Howard Dean instantly lost credibility as a leader. Many political pundits have speculated upon reflection that eventually the campaign was sunk more by the candidate's puffed ego than the sound of his voice, but the two seemed to collide symbolically that frosty night in Iowa.

Dean's ego defined his legacy, and it did anything but propel his political career. His ideas may have been good, but his ego drowned them out. You see, ego is the expression of deeper character issues—ranging from selfishness to inferiority—coming out through unfit communication that will not sustain your ideas or secure your influence. Ego is a megaphone that is always obnoxious.

An overbearing ego dials up the volume until a leader cannot be ignored, but in turn it creates layers of problems for a ministry.

Is Ego an Occupational Hazard for Leaders?

The search committee of a major ministry was ecstatic over the interview with their top candidate. He came into the room with presence, energy, and a command of the challenges. The leader had forceful answers to every question, confronted the committee brashly about the organization's shortcomings, and painted a big-picture vision like they had never seen before, even promising that extravagant grants to the ministry would quickly follow should he be hired. The leader's unwavering confidence is what the board thought they were hiring, but an obnoxious ego is what they got. Within three months, the same board fired the new CEO, leaving the ministry in turmoil for a long time afterward.

Ego in any package is noisy, but it becomes particularly problematic in the hands of leaders. At best, ego that focuses attention on the leader over the mission and the people of the organization is annoying; at worst, it creates a series of serious long-term problems for the ministry.

Some might say that ego is an occupational hazard for leaders. To move successfully into a leadership position, you must have drive, gifting, a track record of success, and a certain level of ambition. Talented, up-and-coming leaders are given responsibilities ahead of their years, and they are praised lavishly for their accomplishments. Thus, by the time they move into the corner office, they may have become convinced that they are superior in many ways to others and that the aggressiveness that got them into the big chair is what is needed to keep them there.

Such factors also provide fertile ground for growing an ego that will dominate all a leader does. Like weeds in a carefully prepared vegetable garden, ego needs to be purposefully eradicated if a leader desires to achieve genuine success and have any hopes of gathering the harvest in the longview.

In his standard-setting study, *Good to Great,* Jim Collins proved to the business world that the best companies all had leaders who were "characterized not by charisma, ego, or larger-than-life celebrity—but by a paradoxical combination of deep humility and intense professional will."[1] If secular businesses can only achieve greatness when the leader is without ego, how much more does that principle apply in the church?

Me Theology

Too much ego has wormed its way into the church through a "me-focused" theology that creates sanctified excuses for self-centeredness and ego. Serving God is not about what is in it for me. It is not about asking Jesus for a shopping list of things that will diminish my troubles. And most importantly, it is not about being lifted up in the eyes of others. Loving and serving God is about glorifying Him. Faithful living is about honoring Christ in what we do. And being a Christian is about living in a way that makes sure our Lord is the center of attention and praise.

In the past few years we've all seen pastors of one megachurch after another leave their positions in disgrace. And when you study those churches, there is always a common characteristic—the ministry was centered in the personality of the messenger rather than the power of the message. Moreover, these self-aggrandizing Christian leaders invariably implemented strong boundaries to assure autonomy and keep others away. Their desire never to share the spotlight, coupled with walls of protection to keep accountability at bay, led to tragic moral failures.

Ego-driven leaders may not believe it, but in a biblical model of ministry, they are pretty far down the list in importance:

1. God
2. The mission
3. The people you serve
4. The team of employees who do the work
5. The leaders who serve the team

The higher four priorities stay fairly constant, but too many Christian leaders are attempting to claw their way up this ladder in an effort to be recognized, and are hindering the work of God in the process. Because ego-driven leadership must be continually fed, it demands that immediate needs are always more important than the longview results, thus stifling opportunity for ministry of lasting value.

Your ministry doesn't need the flair of your inflated ego; rather, it is your authenticity that will most effectively motivate those you serve in leadership. And that genuineness is most often communicated in a soft tone that has no relation to bravado—a well-reasoned argument that can be coupled with passion to get the attention of internal and external constituencies, and a caring and gracious spirit that attracts around it people ready to listen and respond.

Unfortunately, the more flagrant offenders of these principles don't even realize they are doing so. Leaders often develop ego through their experience, get pulled into it for its comfort, or get pushed into it because of erroneous assumptions they make about their role. But in all cases, the end result is that their leadership effectiveness is greatly reduced as they elect to major on the short-term gains of showmanship rather than taking the steady strides of a true statesman.

A Portrait of the Showmen

Based upon research and personal observation, the following is a compilation of traits seen most often in ego-driven leaders. While these patterns are not found in every ego-inflated leader and may not fully capture the uniqueness of each individual, a review of these characteristics may trigger leaders to evaluate whether these patterns are evident and need to be corrected.

Live Flamboyantly

These leaders have convinced themselves that by possessing the best, they lift the stature of their ministry and message. So they live well, appreciate excess, and are drawn to lavishness in things and people, while justifying that as fulfilling their role.

Inflate Vision

They "wow" the people they meet with an ability to articulate an enormous vision, but constantly overpromise and under-deliver because they are not grounded in what is realistic. Their initial contact is impressive, but their track record is littered with those they blame for the failures.

Act Invincible

Their puffed-up ego makes them assume life will get out of their way, and they charge headlong into challenges without awareness of the harm they may bring to themselves or others. Winning becomes more important than being prudent or wise.

Ignore Critics

These leaders find fault with critics, rather than listen to their insights. They tend not only to dismiss the critic's ideas, but also to discredit the messenger to assure hard questions will not take hold and to reclaim the position of one who always "knows best" and has such good ideas that his confidantes need to protect him from future wacko critics attempting to tear him down.

Crave Adrenaline

They have a "go-for-broke" approach to life that assumes they will always beat the odds. Confident their gifts can overcome any obstacle, they gain energy in flagrant risk taking and have concluded the accompanying adrenaline surge validates their value.

Exaggerate Actions

These leaders move in wide, sweeping motions that take up space wherever they might be. They don't do anything simply, but every action is so exaggerated that the staff around them is exhausted, rather than equipped, by their leadership.

Become Sensitive

While these ego-driven leaders can usually dish it out, they can't take it and are thin skinned. They are easily offended and, because they are desperate to be admired, criticism wounds them visibly. They react to attacks swiftly either by countering the action or secluding themselves.

Attract Groupies

Because they want to be lionized, they gather around them people who tend to be inexperienced, weak, and loyal. They want "yes men/women," not peers who might hold them accountable, and they often do so under the guise of "mentoring."

Demand Appreciation

Ego-driven leaders can never seem to get enough attention. Whether it is found in name recognition, an entourage, or bright lights, these leaders make their decisions based on what will meet this craving for recognition.

Require Empathy

Recognition and appreciation are not enough for these ego-based leaders; they also demand that others understand and empathize with the "pressure, sacrifices, and loneliness" of leadership. Ironically, these same leaders are often unable to be empathetic to others.

Listen Poorly

Their ego seems to block their ability to listen, because they assume they are the smartest people in the room. They want to be heard, not instructed, and thus their listening skills have never been developed.

Enjoy Competition

These are people who are competitive for the sake of getting ahead of others. Blinded to the greater good, they seek the recognition that comes from winning, rather than the satisfaction that comes from mission fulfillment.

Control Obsessively

In the name of stewardship or service, these leaders tend to control everything with meticulous detail. They are uncomfortable in situations where they are not in charge, and so tend to avoid those invitations.

Ignore Boundaries

These leaders live as if the boundaries that apply to others are inconsequential to them. They assume worth is brought to the ministry by shattering the limits, and justify their personal overstepping by citing the demands, calling, and value of their leadership.

Of course not every showman's portrait is the same, and certainly some of these characteristics are less egregious—we all wince slightly at the leader whose vanity leads him to set a meeting date as if he were granting an audience with the king. Other times the level of pomp is intolerable—I was once in the office of a leader who actually put his desk up on a platform so that he could "better listen to the staff" during meetings. Sadly, many ego-driven leaders can't imagine the laughable spectacle they are projecting to others.

A Portrait of the Statesmen

The antithesis of an ego-driven leader is the statesman. This is not a role that comes by way of position; it is rooted in character. Far from aspiring to it, such stature comes to leaders as they grow and mature in leadership that is grounded in respect earned over an extended time. They are comfortable in themselves, have nothing to prove, and are not seeking anything beyond what God has currently given them.

Length of service alone does not make a statesman. While lengthy, proven leadership is an important component, there are many long-term leaders who never become statesmen. Unchecked ego-driven leadership patterns usually don't change simply because a leader has arrived at the final job.

True statesmen leaders are so secure they don't need to accentuate the power differential between themselves and others in order to lead, and in fact seek to minimize the gap. At the same time, they do not try to be "one of the boys," giving up their leadership responsibility. Rather, they lead with wisdom, service, maturity, caring, and gentle presence. They seek to lift others up, rather than push them down, and travel further by equipping others to go ahead of them.

Statesmen push the attention outward rather than drawing it inward. They seek to broaden circles of access rather than restrict them, and include others rather than create false barriers that only a select few are allowed to cross. These leaders are always learning, drawing out other people's new perspectives, information, and ideas. They believe the reflections of others are to be enjoyed, not endured until it's time to "give the right answer." They ask more questions than they answer, adapt to the ways of others, and are continually growing rather than clinging to self-sufficient wisdom.

Beyond simply listening to the concerns and insights of others, they have the ability to connect the emotional ties, rather than just the facts, in order to create a meaningful relationship—they empathize. Statesmen calmly pull others to them through their accepting spirit. They have purposefully developed a pattern of patience that accepts with ease the shortcomings, pace, or learning curve of others.

These are stark contrasts between the showman and the Christian statesman, but the summary is not as harsh as the Scripture on this topic: "Pride ends in humiliation, while humility brings honor," declares Proverbs 29:23. There is no more accurate synopsis of the difference between these two types of leaders: One falls over time, and the other is lifted up in the view of others and, most importantly, in the eyes of God. The true statesman takes the longview, foregoing the short-burn tactics of showmanship altogether. He builds his house on the rock foundation of his personal character, not on the sand of ego.

Removing Ego from Leadership

For those who have read far enough into this discussion to discover they need to deal with ego issues, four steps are critical to moving out of a destructive ego-driven leadership pattern. The most important link in this healing comes just by knowing there is a problem, and heart-changed leaders who realize they need to adjust their ways are far ahead of the pack.

Keep Quiet

One of the greatest challenges for ego-driven leaders is to keep quiet. They establish their presence by talking, monopolizing the discussion because they are convinced their leadership role requires them to be adding value to every encounter with coworkers. In doing this, the leader not only keeps the goal from being reached, but also significantly devalues employees and lessens their commitment.

Thus, for example, when an employee comes with an idea about which he or she is excited, ego-centered leaders want to add to the idea, instead of focusing on the accomplishment. They may improve it a bit, but they also dramatically deflate the desire of the employee to see the idea properly carried out. Leaders have to ask if what they add is really worth the cost, because often it is not.

This same call to quietness is true for meetings. I learned long ago, if you wait long enough in meetings, someone else will eventually say what you are thinking. If no one does, you can always add it in later in a statesmanlike way. But speaking first or often to establish position or prove your expertise is not a good reason to take up time in a meeting.

Scripture instructs ego-driven leaders directly and boldly, and the words of Romans need no interpretation: "Live in harmony with each other. Don't be too proud to enjoy the company of ordinary people. And don't think you know it all!" (12:16). Leaders who struggle with ego issues would do well to begin by being quiet, allowing time for the reverberation of their egos to fade.

Seek Balance

When successful leaders "believe their own press," it creates in them the illusion of single-handedly being responsible for the successes. Thus, when ego-prone leaders find the limelight and become more visible and celebrated, they have a proclivity to forget the other factors that made the advances possible. The accolades of others blur perspective about their own talents and encourage the belief that anything they do in the future will be equally successful, perhaps even more so.

Ego-stimulated leaders live out of balance because in their desire to attract attention, they have created a persona that is fragile and cannot withstand examination—the reason they attempt to keep others at arm's length through their bluster. Measuring personal and professional value by the accolades they receive, they live in jealous fear that someone more attractive will steal their spotlight. Moreover, by confusing themselves with their personas, ego-driven leaders never reach the full potential of what God Himself created them to be.

In contrast, the balanced leader looks in the mirror rather than watching out the window to see who might be coming. Statesmen never attempt to measure up to unrealistic expectations. They find joy and balance through regularly examining their own lives to assure they stay genuine to how God has gifted them. These leaders are content "living in their own skin" and stay there through systematic examination of their own character, attitudes, and motives.

Proverbs again addresses this pattern, reminding us, "A peaceful heart leads to a healthy body; jealousy is like cancer in the bones" (14:30). And *Harvard Business Review* studied the same phenomenon, concluding, "Those who make it to the top—and stay there peacefully—all share a remarkable sense of proportion

and a high degree of self-awareness, despite widely different personality and management styles. Their secret? Powerfully modest
habits of mind and behavior."[2]

There are few who can accurately self-evaluate. In repeated
studies, most people rate themselves much higher than their true
skills. And thus, leaders need at least one person who will shoot
absolutely straight with them and be both their best friend and
best critic. Remarkably, among the statesmen I've enjoyed working
with, that person is nearly always their spouse.

Ambition Is Okay

While evaluating the pitfalls of an ego-driven leader, it is
important not to lose sight of a critical factor of success that can
be wrapped up in the ego discussion: Namely, there is a significant
difference between big ego and big ambition. Both may achieve
the same goals, but the first is motivated by the attention it will
bring to the leader, while the second is driven by the advances
it will bring to the ministry. All leaders must be ambitious to be
successful, but those who can find the right balance between their
personal vision and that of the greater good are the ones who will
be successful long term.

Confront Sin

There is no wiggle room when addressing pride that is the root
of a leader's ego. It is sin, no matter how you cut it.

Jesus identifies pride among a list of what we consider especially ugly sins: "Out of a person's heart, come evil thoughts, sexual

immorality, theft, murder, adultery, greed, wickedness, deceit, lustful desires, envy, slander, pride, and foolishness" (Mark 7:21–22).

The leaders God blessed repented of their pride: "Then Hezekiah humbled himself and repented of his pride, as did the people of Jerusalem. So the LORD's anger did not fall on them during Hezekiah's lifetime" (2 Chron. 32:26).

Christian statesman John Stott writes, "Pride, then, is more than the first of the seven deadly sins; it is itself the essence of all sin. For it is the stubborn refusal to let God be God, with the corresponding ambition to take his place. It is the attempt to dethrone God and enthrone ourselves. Sin is self-deification."[3]

Pastor Rick Warren expresses the same tone, saying, "I think the worst sin is pride. In fact, the Bible says it. The Bible says that pride is the worst sin. It is, as the Bible says, it's the sin that got Satan kicked out of heaven.… Pride goes before destruction."[4]

The challenges of an ego-driven leader are not solved through the retooling of leadership gifts. Only at the foot of the cross in repentance can God bring about genuine change: "Human pride will be brought down, and human arrogance will be humbled. Only the LORD will be exalted" (Isa. 2:11).

Who you are as a person when no one is looking is more important than the most public thing you will ever do in leadership. Godly leaders have overcome the roots of sin that allow their ego to dominate their leadership. They have done the hard work it takes over years to personally become less so that Jesus can be more in their lives. While keeping strong their God-given ambition, they have assured that pride cannot take root to erode the future of their ministry. These longview leaders have made a personal investment and have built accountability into their relationships to assure they are developing a God-honoring character as the first requirement of their responsibility to those they serve as leader.

3

Applause Lasts for a Moment,
but Leadership Is for a Lifetime

Forty-six percent of employees surveyed by HotJobs.com said a willingness to share responsibility and credit is the most important hallmark of a good boss.[1] That's nearly double the percentage of those who valued the next most important attribute—mentoring. Is it not odd, then, that the staple obsession of business trade magazines is "How to Get the Attention of Your Boss"?

The energy that employees focus upon gaining recognition has become inordinately skewed, even while they most appreciate a leader who doles out recognition generously. We must address the dysfunction directly by being leaders who understand how to give away the credit and shoulder the bad news ourselves. Those who fail at this core quality of leadership have lost touch with the people on the front lines of ministry, and perhaps more important, will never work past the immediacy of their selfish needs in order to lead for the longview.

Why is this? Because giving away the credit never hurts a leader in the long run, but hoarding the credit always does. Good leaders share or better yet totally give away credit for the positive things that happen, knowing it will ultimately circle back around to strengthen their own worth to the organization. And when negative results need to be shouldered, good leaders don't place the blame on others—who may rightly deserve it—but carry that load alone.

Unfortunately, leadership is filled with people who want more and more recognition, even at the cost of those under their care. Inevitably, those who do take the wrong path of placing blame find they may deflect criticism in the short run, but they will be weakened over time, as the grapevine retelling of the story will cast the leader (fairly or not) as one who shirks personal responsibility.

Leadership Stop Sign

Christian leaders need to get past the need for recognition. You already get enough of the spotlight because of your position, presence, and role in the ministry; you don't need to be looking for more. Not only is it unhealthy organizationally, it is not biblical. The Bible gives clear instruction in Ephesians 6:6–9 about the importance of leadership that gives away the credit and shoulders bad news. For my own guidance, I've contextualized this Scripture to apply it to my life as a leader:

> *Leadership is not about honoring you; its only purpose is fulfilling God's calling. You should work hard, but if you're doing it because others will recognize and appreciate you, then you don't understand the type of servant leadership to which God has called you. When your passion for Christ is so ingrained with your work,*

you realize how unimportant the recognition of others becomes in contrast to being responsible to the Lord. Leaders don't need to rob recognition from those under their care, because it is the Lord who rewards us. In honoring your employees, you lift them up as people of high value in the eyes of the Lord. You never have the right to treat employees inappropriately and look down on them, because the leader is equal to them in God's eyes, and you both serve the same leader—Christ Jesus, who doesn't favor anyone.

Here it is on a stop sign: Leader, you already receive more credit and status than 95 percent of the people in your network will see in a lifetime, so be satisfied and stop looking for more!

Instead, develop a heart of genuine gratitude as you move through your ministry, and you'll see the world through the eyes of your employees—and make your ministry infinitely more effective on the whole. Your coworkers will become more committed and more mission focused when their leader values them as God values them and doesn't weigh them down with the burden of blame for their mistakes. Beyond this, your legacy as their leader will be one of godly deference, rather than attention grabbing or blame shifting for quick gains in approval ratings.

The Gratitude Equation

As children we are conditioned to seek approval for each individual task, from passing our spelling tests to cleaning our rooms to washing our hands for dinner. From those earliest years we learn to seek credit for meeting the expectations of parents, teachers, or others in authority over us. Of course as we mature, we learn to check our need to be recognized audibly for each success, although privately we still hope someone applauds our achievements. That ingrained childhood pattern continues into the workplace, where we are drawn to want a "grade for every paper" like we had in school. We're not satisfied with a report at the end of the term but find comfort in the immediate feedback of the moment.

When I was pastoring a church in Detroit, I didn't feel the need to be recognized by those going out the door who may have felt obligated to compliment the preacher on the sermon. But after the church was empty and we were headed to lunch, I waited in anguished anticipation until I heard my wife—my best critic—say the message was okay. In our adult life we shouldn't need recognition and ought to be happy with the satisfaction we did our best, but the acknowledgment of those around us still matters—and we continue to seek it.

The efficacy of sharing the credit and accepting the blame goes far beyond making someone's day because they were praised or not scolded. The motivation, creativity, and commitment of workers increase dramatically when they feel they are valued. Even their health improves: British researchers report that workers who believe their bosses treated them unfairly had a 30 percent higher rate of coronary heart disease after ten years; labor experts believe "the toll taken on employees' health might be even greater in the

United States than in Britain, since workers in the U.S. spend more time at their jobs than their counterparts overseas."[2] If a secure leader can impact a worker's physical heart, imagine how much more his positive behavior can affect the heart emotionally and spiritually.

Giving gratitude is key to fostering contentment in the workplace and happiness in the other areas of life. Studies have found that people who made a daily and/or frequent practice of being thankful were "not only more joyful; they were healthier, less stressed, more optimistic, and more likely to help others."[3]

Receiving recognition builds us up. It assures us in our gifts. It creates a healthful comfort zone of operation. Maybe God wired us with this need for recognition and acceptance so we would be drawn into families and communities. It is not sinful to want to be appreciated, but it can become just that when it is more important to us than the acceptance of God.

Building Credit Accounts

In leadership, our need for appreciation must shift to an entirely different level. In sum, leaders build up recognition over time, while others earn their credit for participation in individual events. A good leader must grasp the difference and act accordingly.

Idiosyncratic credit theory is a primary organizational premise used to evaluate the transactional nature of leadership. First developed by E. P. Hollander in 1956 to explain why the idiosyncratic traits of leaders are tolerated, the theory essentially suggests every employee comes into the workplace with a "zero credit" balance. Through "positive contributions" of successes, styles, and skills, each of us builds up credit—or through negative action creates a deficit. The ramifications of this model are extensive in explaining the uniqueness of leadership.

Leaders build their credit balance, or deficit, slowly, over time. A short-term leader who has yet to build up positive credit will be severely criticized for a blunder, while that same mistake will be brushed aside if made by a long-term leader with a strong positive credit balance. Leaders who have accumulated a "deep deficit" in their credit account are unlikely to ever dig out of that hole, no matter how many positive things they may do in the future.

Thinking of this process as a bank account demonstrates how leaders with a large account have such freedom, while those in arrears have little room to operate:

(1) As a leader builds up the individual "credit accounts" of his or her coworkers, the leader makes the team more successful, and in turn, the leader's "credit account" is also strengthened.

(2) Leaders who have built up positive responses over time are "forgiven" easily for a blunder because they have already established a large reserve of positive credit.

The strongest leaders find that the investments and dividends of giving the credit away multiply back to them over time. Leaders who function with this understanding create a strong positive credit balance over time that can be "spent" to weather storms, explore innovative ideas, or tackle objectives that will only be reached with persistent long-term effort.

Understanding and living in this framework should release even the most stingy leaders to give away credit freely to others. There is just not a downside to giving away all the credit to those who are on the front lines of ministry work.

Six Principles of Giving Away the Credit

Once we understand how leaders are uniquely measured within a ministry, it is important to give others credit in ways that are appropriate, and resist the temptation to give praise without actually releasing the credit from a leader's hand.

Be Purposeful

Leaders move at a fast pace, and it is easy to overlook those who have earned recognition. Looking for opportunities to give away credit is the first and most critical step in developing this leadership trait. A helpful exercise is to designate a day to keep a list of every instance when you could have shown appreciation to others. If you did them all, you probably would get nothing else accomplished, but just tracking the opportunities during a single day will help build awareness of the moments when you could thank those around you.

If you don't train your vision to notice these times, you will become hardened to the opportunities to give credit away and not see them even when they hit you head-on. It is remarkable to me how often ministry employees say about their supervisor, "If you're waiting to be thanked, you'll wait a long time." Some leaders are just oblivious to the opportunity to give away the credit, and so they never do.

Be Poignant

Giving credit that is not genuine is worse than being silent, because hollow appreciation is destructive in the long term. Instead, gratitude must come from the heart and be credible through and through. While a leader may genuinely appreciate a colleague, praise expressed in repetitive reactions rather than meaningful responses becomes pointless at best and a source of contempt at worst.

As I was talking with a ministry leader in his office one day, a worker interrupted us to bring needed documents. My friend stopped our conversation to praise the delivery person, saying, "You're the most valuable person in the world to me right now." I was impressed with his expression and the way in which he underscored the importance of getting the material quickly. But I was surprised when the worker didn't even smile in return. As our day of meetings progressed, I understood why—for the leader said the exact same thing to nearly everyone we encountered, and more than one walked away suppressing a smirk.

Be Personal

Giving the credit means little when it is systematized, programmed, or predictable. An employee of the month program is a perfect example of impersonal appreciation. In a small organization, it becomes a rotating honor among the limited group. In a middle-size organization, it becomes a point of jealousy and petty judgmentalism. In a large ministry, it becomes meaningless because the employees don't all know each other. Leaders tend to gravitate toward an "award" credit structure because it keeps the focus as much on the one who is making the selection as it does on the employee being appreciated.

To give credit away meaningfully, leaders need to personalize the recognition they give and express it when it is not expected. Telephone calls, emails, and sidewalk chats are all simple and effective ways to thank those with whom you work. I often use handwritten note cards to send a word of encouragement. A "walk-about" in your offices offers opportunities to personally inquire about the priorities in various individuals' work and focus that discussion on your thankfulness for the contributions they make.

But no matter the method of expressing recognition, it must be personal. I've heard employees who work with some of the Christian world's busiest leaders say, "When he talks to me, it seems like he has nothing else to do than be concerned about me." That is the kind of personal attention that our ministry colleagues deserve.

Be Pure

Coworkers will see through any attempt to give away credit if the leader's intention is self-serving. A frequent example of this attention-grabbing effort is the leader who attempts to be a "regular person" and work alongside frontline employees in order to demonstrate valuing others. That is well and good if genuine. But shame on the leader who dons the tall chef's hat at the ministry Fourth of July picnic to cook hot dogs just so everyone will notice. Likewise, college presidents are notorious for carrying a few suitcases on freshman move-in day, but usually just long enough to get their picture taken for the school magazine.

While it is probably best to stay out of that arena unless it fits your established style, leaders who want to show appreciation for the work of others by sharing in their task need to join in the tough jobs rather than cherry-picking opportunities to bring the attention back to themselves. JetBlue former CEO and founder David Neeleman did it right when flying on his airplanes, by becoming just one of the crew members—passing out snacks and cleaning the airplane after the passengers disembark. There was a direct correlation between his willingness to demonstrate appreciation by working alongside his team in the dirty, unseen jobs and the airline being ranked first in customer service.

Be Prerequisite-Free

I had the opportunity to hear unvarnished reports from inside a ministry whose leader is well known by his employees as one who gives away credit—but does it in ways that obligate them to the leader, constrain their objective perspectives, and create jealousy among the ranks. Instead of thanking people, he enjoyed playing the role of "candy man," expressing his gratitude with gifts and trips. While the lavish perks were a surprise bonus the first few times, the "attention of the king" (as it was secretly called) became a source of division and ridicule among the workers. It sure doesn't create ministry cohesion when only a few are talking about their new iPod or their trip to Hawaii.

Leaders should give of themselves, not give things. There is little good that ever comes from giving gifts to donors or employees.

If donors wanted a gift, they could have bought their own, and if employees need a raise, then give them one, but don't present a gift that accentuates the power differential between the leader and others. Plus, it is hard to encourage financial restraint in budget spending when the leader is tossing out trinkets like the grand marshal of a Mardi Gras parade. This practice does not honor coworkers but rather seeks only to focus attention on the giver of the prequisites.

Be Prayerful

Leaders who develop the pattern of praying for those whom they appreciate will find that God will open even more genuine opportunities to give the credit to others and bring a meaningful boost to their lives. A prayerful spirit in our gratitude keeps our motives in check, reminds us of our equal position in God's eyes, and assures that our expressions of gratitude come to our coworkers unencumbered.

Leaders should be sensitive to pray for their people in a way that fits the other person's comfort zone. Some may welcome a time of intense prayer in the hallway, and others would melt in embarrassment if included in that prayer. But whether privately or with the coworker, it is amazing how support in prayer puts an exclamation point of correct emphasis on a team member's accomplishment so that the glory is given to God.

Breaking the childhood pattern of craving individual credit and, in turn, giving it away freely is the first step for leaders. The second is learning to shoulder bad news, rather than placing blame.

Broad Shoulders Carry Bad News

A popular poster from the satirical Despair.com reads, "The secret to success is knowing who to blame for your failures." And placing blame on those whom God has entrusted to us in ministry is just about that blatantly silly.

The context of my modified idiosyncratic credit theory is again the framework for understanding why leaders can more easily shoulder the weight of bad news. If a leader has built up a reserve balance of goodwill, the credit balance will remain positive despite the negative news—while employees who measure their worth by evaluation of each task do not have that luxury, so to place blame on them becomes devastating. Furthermore, the leader who takes the burden of bad news will be respected and trusted in the long run and is best equipped to offer comfort in time of crisis.

Leaders should use three tools for sharing bad news without placing blame.

Be Direct

Every spouse of a soldier killed in battle knows that the bad news is delivered the second two officers in dress military uniforms pull into the driveway. There is no gentle way to break bad news, and in a ministry, slowing that process only accentuates the difficulty of dealing with the challenges. Bad news needs to be shared quickly—but not until all the facts can be gathered so that the leader is assured the analysis of the situation is clear.

Occasionally leaders will rush this stage of the process to run forward with bad news before the assessment is complete, but doing so creates mistrust if the information is not reliable. The more typical pattern of leaders is to shield the bad news from others with the hope and prayer that a solution can be found before the circumstances become public. Every situation is unique, but those under your care are part of the solution to any problem, and they are most likely to be responsive when brought into the discussion early rather than being held at arm's length.

Be Disclosing

When sharing a difficult challenge, we owe it to our ministry coworkers to shoot straight with them. The *Apollo 13* spacecraft trouble became known to the world with the infamous words "Houston, we have a problem …"—and that is the correct way to start the explanation. Don't sugarcoat, underplay, or discount the fullness of your challenge. This is the time when others need to feel confident they know as much as the leader about the challenge.

Good news can be leaked, allowing it to spread across your ministry team because it is likely to retain its integrity of factual base. But bad news must be announced, or the gossip and speculation will run far ahead of the facts. In tough moments some leaders want to share bad news only with their trusted team and shield others in the ministry from the challenge. The flaw in this approach is that the news will leak out, and when it does, it spreads like wildfire. I don't bring my entire employee base together lightly, because I figure it costs us about $10,000 an hour in wages when we gather, but the cost of not meeting during a time of bad news is much higher. Without the full story, coworkers become fearful, assumptions run rampant, and energy is drained by the uncertainty. Leaders may have learned to live comfortably with a high level of ambiguity, but others have not.

Leadership in a time of crisis demands we create a genuine "no spin zone" and present the facts as fully and accurately as we can. A leader who cannot define reality cannot be trusted to find a viable answer. If others believe you are hiding something, your coworkers rightfully will press for further information and be cautious of the resolutions presented—especially any involving sacrifice on their part. You don't have to have all the answers to share problems transparently, because your coworkers will trust you in the solution if you don't disguise the struggle ahead.

Be Discreet

It is important to understand the difference between correcting and blaming—the first is done in private, and the second occurs in public. Leaders must privately correct those who make mistakes, and create personal growth plans to assure coworkers learn to fulfill their responsibilities. Part of that plan entails the leader forgiving them for the mistake so they can get a fresh start and move forward rather than being weighed down by their errors. This is much different from pointing out the flaws of others publicly.

I know two leaders in the same town who lead nearly identical-size ministries—both of whom faced a serious financial crisis that was created by an error of their respective chief financial officers. One leader called in the CFO and took strong action privately to assure the problem would not recur, then pulled together the entire staff to explain the problem, never mentioning the CFO. The other president called together his team, his board members, and the newspaper to identify the finance officer as the source of the problem, to explain the problem and make it clear that the president knew nothing of the misguided accounting practices. Both CFOs did eventually wind up being fired because they were ill equipped for the job, but the first CEO was thriving two years later, and the second had been pushed out of office. It never pays for leaders to place blame.

Ultimately, leaders must learn that shouldering blame and giving away credit won't hurt them long term. But even if it does, the Bible clearly guides us on this point: "Remember, it is better to suffer for doing good, if that is what God wants, than to suffer for doing wrong!" (1 Peter 3:17).

Blaming others is never the correct action: "You know that the rulers in this world lord it over their people, and officials flaunt their authority over those under them" (Mark 10:42).

Giving away credit and shouldering bad news may rub against your natural instincts and even some of your training, but it is the most important habit for a leader to cultivate if the full potential of a ministry is to be unleashed. When you step out of the spotlight and into the shop where real leadership gets done, you begin to build up the credit you need to be effective for the duration.

4

Vulnerability May Get You in, but Humility Keeps You There

A pastor who shares on Sunday morning the details of his lengthy, ongoing battle with a sinful habit may make the congregation feel better about their own struggles with demons. But exposing himself in order to demonstrate vulnerability diminishes his ability to be sought out as a counselor who can be looked to for advice.

A school leader who wears a baseball cap backward, plays ping-pong every day after lunch, and "chills" with the students in order to not appear haughty around them may gain short-term accolades as accessible. But when a tough student-discipline decision awaits, it is not a "buddy" in whom students and parents want to entrust their future.

A ministry leader may feel she is connecting with the team by sharing the personal turmoil, burdens, and uncertainties of leadership in order to come across as one of the crowd. But instead, she raises unspoken questions about trusting the one who makes the key decisions of finance, direction, and personnel.

While pride is an unattractive quality in leaders, humility is a strength that compels others to follow. In an effort to be seen as humble, many leaders have wrongfully substituted vulnerability for humility, and in doing so turned a self-centered spotlight on themselves, laying the groundwork for leadership deterioration. Coworkers may desire the immediacy of equality that results when a leader exposes his needs and shortcomings, or the leader may seek personal acceptance from others by appearing vulnerable.

Leaders are not free from genuine vulnerabilities—they are real people who have doubts, fears, shortcomings, and challenges just like everyone else—but those are issues that must not be intermingled with the workplace. (This is one of the prices paid to carry the responsibility of leadership.) Leaders who purposefully expose their liabilities limit their sphere of influence and often forfeit their long-term viability. Confidence in the leader will be lessened at best, and at worst, the workers will eventually use those "chinks in the armor" to attack the leader at a point of vulnerability. Humility and vulnerability are two different things, and the first must be established without offering the second.

Vulnerability Is a Cheap Imitation of Humility

Substituting vulnerability for humility is often a sign of serious underlying personal issues. In the 1980s, then-president Richard Berendzen of American University in Washington DC, wrote a diary-form account of life as a university president in a book titled *Is My Armor Straight?* His book was heralded as a great show of vulnerability to allow others to see past the veneer of the presidency and let the world understand the real, behind-the-scenes struggles of high-profile leadership.

The autobiography was filled with stories that appeared to make him look vulnerable, but in actuality, it was an obnoxious puff piece. The overwhelming "poor me" attitude of the book was overlaid on the details of his daily work—from budget challenges to union contracts to hosting world leaders. He uses the metaphor of a suit of armor to reflect how vulnerable he felt. Sadly, three years after the book's release Richard Berendzen pleaded guilty to charges of making obscene phone calls from his president's office to a woman, talking about the sexual acts he wanted to perform on young children—he left that "vulnerability" out of the book.

Of course, not every leader who shows vulnerability is hiding a deeper problem, but too often it is a reliable pattern. The examples of Jim Bakker and Jimmy Swaggart are infamous, both television preachers praised for being a new brand of Christian leader who were willing to be vulnerable, but of course, both hiding dark secrets. This pattern of showing vulnerability before a moral collapse has been repeated in scores of Christian leaders.

Expressing vulnerability can be a style issue without any lurking issues, especially with younger leaders who have been developed with a more open approach. But leaders who wish to come across as vulnerable are often ego centered and thus prone to more serious problems because their attempt to be vulnerable deflects attention from an internal or external probing of more serious issues.

Chinks in the Armor

Although his ego-driven motives were misguided, Richard Berendzen's metaphor of armor is sometimes an appropriate way to describe leadership, because there are battles for which leaders must be well protected. Leadership demands hard decisions, and even the best listening, most responsive, and articulately persuasive leaders cannot please everyone. The risk of attack remains even when success is demonstrated. Why, then, should any leader further increase their susceptibility by shows of vulnerability, especially knowing they may well be undermining their own hard-won gains?

Generally, leaders resort to "letting down their guard" at the very moment when they should be leveraging the credibility they have established by proven integrity.

Guiding a ministry through eighteen years of dramatic growth, a leader produced significant increases in reach, stature, and strength for the ministry. Along the way, he had to upset some who liked it "how it used to be," and others became disgruntled over their dissatisfaction with specific issues—although none could deny the overall success.

Being confident in his long-term leadership role but wanting to find new ways to connect with his team, he began to be purposefully more vulnerable, sharing with others the struggles of an attack he was facing from a disgruntled employee. Those he opened up to agreed he'd made the right decision to fire the former worker, and he began to enjoy the reinforcement that came with letting down his guard to be transparent about the toll it had taken on him.

But it didn't take long for his naysayers to begin circulating rumors that the leader was expressing to others how fatigued he had become, which grew into them watching carefully to exaggerate any quick reaction of the leader as "irritability" and then "instability." The question of "trust" soon began to circulate, and then many decisions over the previous years began to be reexamined around lunchroom tables, then conference room tables, and eventually the boardroom table.

It took less than a year from his first "show of vulnerability" until the CEO was fired, because the board felt "he needed a break from the stress of leadership." The accumulation of bumps and bruises through years of leadership brought about the firing, but because of his strong track record, his opponents couldn't attack in response to their real frustrations. They needed to wait to find a legitimate chink in the leader's armor.

While a show of vulnerability brings with it immediate gratification for a leader seeking support, it also attracts critics in the same way blood in the water attracts sharks ready to attack. One of my looming concerns for leadership in today's environment is the difficulty of remaining at one ministry for a significant length of time. One of the reasons for this is leaders' increasing tendency to resort to these shortsighted quests for camaraderie among those they seek to lead. Leaders who wish to go the distance must learn to reject the empty promise of "transparency" before their critics make it out to be a disqualifying fault.

The Crown of Humility

Humility is a character trait of a completely different order than vulnerability, and every leader should become humble. Humility is essential for effective leadership, and it is the base of the biblical model for leaders: "'God opposes the proud but favors the humble.' So humble yourselves under the mighty power of God, and at the right time he will lift you up in honor" (1 Peter 5:5–6). Consider that the humility of Jesus exponentially increased His effectiveness as a leader.

Jesus was the most humble person to ever walk this earth. He was God in the body of a human, and He could have done anything He wanted to do—possessing the power to make anything happen. But He limited Himself to only what His heavenly Father asked Him to do. And so through His humility, Jesus was able to spend ordinary days with His disciples and reveal the nature of God to them through a deep mentoring relationship.

Maybe they exist, but I've never seen a Christian who is prideful be a meaningful mentor. The marvelous theologian J. I. Packer writes, "It is impossible at the same time to give the impression both that I am a great Christian and that Jesus Christ is a great Master."[1] Mentoring is not about having answers for those who come to sit at our feet, for the Christian life is not adopting a set of simplistic patterns. No, genuine mentoring is listening more than lecturing, praying more than preaching, and caring more than curing. It is trusting that God will be lifted up instead of ourselves as we invest in coworkers. This kind of humility—grounded in a core worldview of respect for the gifts of God for talent and position—is the key ingredient to delivering great mentoring to those you lead. In fact some of the greatest companies in the world have discovered this very thing.

The Key to Greatness

In the insightful study of Jim Collins in his 2001 book *Good to Great,* he and his research team evaluated the "good" companies that had become "great" companies. They defined the "great" as those who had stock returns at least three times the market rate for fifteen years after a major transition period. Collins reports that among the 1,435 Fortune 500 companies studied, only eleven had achieved "greatness."

These findings shocked the researchers who discovered that what these companies had in common were what Collins defines as "Level 5 Leadership, characterized not by charisma, ego, or larger than life celebrity—but by a paradoxical combination of deep humility and intense professional will."[2] The research reported more specifically:

> These Level 5 leaders don't talk about themselves. They'd go on and on about the company and the contributions of other executives, but they would instinctively deflect discussion about their own role. When pressed to talk about themselves, they would say things like, "I hope I'm not sounding like a big shot," or "I don't think I can take much credit for what happened. We were blessed with marvelous people."[3]

Not a single company has become "great" without a genuinely humble leader—who is internally driven by their calling. If true for the secular business world, how much more compelling is the demand for humility in ministry leadership?

Teachability Trumps Power

Perhaps the siren call of vulnerability is so strong to today's leaders because they do not see a viable alternative to lessen the power differentials that separate them from their coworkers. Power has been the most deeply studied tool of leadership because those with power can reward or deprive those who have less power—they can make a day at work wonderful or horrible, and they can enrich or abandon others. The previous generation of leaders accentuated the power held over others—"power differential"—in an attempt to solidify their leadership position. Today's leaders are seeking to free themselves from the stigma of power by substituting vulnerability, but I would suggest that instead, a proper understanding of power is critical for effective, lasting leadership.

Every level of research into the role of power concludes leaders become more effective when they initiate the minimizing of power differentials. The definition of leadership from research developed by the Department of the Navy and published by its director, T. O. Jacobs, has guided me through the years and hits to the heart of this issue: "Leadership is characterized by avoidance of direct confrontations, and is based on the interpersonal interaction skills required to move persons and groups toward goals without interactions that make evident power or status differentials."[4]

While the topic of power encompasses mountains of study by others, I have found in boiling it all down that leaders in ministry who maintain a teachable spirit tend to minimize power differentials, and those who don't, accentuate their power.

I once asked a top ministry executive-search leader what is the most important characteristic he looks for when finding CEOs. Without hesitation he said, "A teachable spirit." He went on to share that leaders willing to learn from those around them are likely to grow and serve well, but leaders who have stopped learning from coworkers have hit their peak of effectiveness. Approaching those you lead with a genuine desire to learn from them rather than playing on their sympathies in shows of vulnerability is the right way to reach out.

Sustaining Teachability

So we see that a good leader must be a humble mentor with a teachable spirit, but what is at the core of a leader's heart and mind? Beyond their communication skills and professional training, a leader must exhibit emotional intelligence.

When the world discovered IQ tests a century ago, measuring intellectual capacity became a driver for schools as well as workplaces. Although now measured in more subtle forms, valuing intelligent workers has shaped the free-floating independence of organizational structure of today—giving smart people room to be effective. This focus is on target because we need bright people to achieve at high levels.

But this quest for brilliance has often ratcheted up the dysfunction in organizations as we've discovered that intelligence doesn't necessarily make one "smart." A Mensa meeting may be the worst place to solve a practical problem, because although the collective IQs are off the chart, the street smarts, or intuition and common sense of the group, are often comparatively low. Those who have excelled academically have not been pressed to develop what has become defined as "emotional intelligence" (EI).

Daniel Goleman, in his 1995 book *Emotional Intelligence: Why It Can Matter More Than IQ,* outlines the five essentials of EI, which clearly demands a level of genuine humility lacing these characteristics together: self-awareness—knowing your strengths and weaknesses; self-regulation—controlling your emotions; motivation—relishing achievement for its own sake; empathy— sensing others' feelings; social skill—building rapport with others.

Goleman argues from his research, "If your emotional abilities aren't in hand, if you don't have self-awareness, if you are not able to manage your distressing emotions, if you can't have empathy and have effective relationships, then no matter how smart you are, you are not going to get very far."[5]

As followers of Christ it is critical for us to grasp the link between the genuine humility of emotional intelligence described by Goldman and the calling on our lives as Christians. Our aim as followers of Christ is to "be mature in the Lord, measuring up to the full and complete standard of Christ" (Eph. 4:13). So what does Christian maturity look like? It looks like Christ-transforming humility grounded in emotional intelligence.

Speaking to the most intellectual community of His day, Jesus summarized our call to maturity by explaining the concept in terms of emotional intelligence, not just intellectual pursuits:

> *"You must love the LORD your God with all your heart, all your soul, and all your mind." This is the first and*

greatest commandment. A second is equally important:
"Love your neighbor as yourself." (Matt. 22:37–39)

This exchange is recorded so we would make no mistake: Love is the calling for all of God's people, and our brightest minds cannot substitute for godly love. Quaker theologian, scholar, and Stanford professor Elton Trueblood has said, "I do not want to be primarily remembered as a Christian scholar, but rather as a loving person."[6]

Loving God and others cannot be segmented in our lives and restricted only to our comfort zones, because it requires our emotions (heart), our spirit (soul), and our intellect (mind). Christian maturity is growing in love for God and others because we understand the sovereign nature of God and our calling to serve the world in His name and way—measuring up to the full stature of Christ. Christian immaturity, on the other hand, is to love God and others because of what is in it for me—living only in the shadow of God's desire for us.

The Inner Strength of a Leader

As we consider accepting our highest calling as Christian leaders—imitating Jesus Christ—we find ourselves desiring to leave behind our own tactics entirely. It is challenging to ask how can we be like Jesus, because He was fully God on earth. Yes, He was, but He also was fully human. And focusing on those human traits that were God filled, we have a clear picture of a mature faith. So what did Jesus do all day? The short answer is that Jesus spent time building

His inner strength so that outwardly He could reveal the nature of God through what He did.

Everything He did with others reflected the nature of God—from the work He did alongside Joseph as a carpenter's apprentice to preaching the Sermon on the Mount. From conversation over a meal to struggling with fatigue from the business of a day to the way He developed relationships—it was all about showing others who God is.

All outward actions in the life of Jesus grew from an inward spiritual strength, and likewise we can't focus on the outcome of revealing the nature of God without linking it to the indwelling of God in our heart, soul, and mind. Beyond the humility we examined earlier, there are four additional center points of inward strength that prepared Jesus for godly leadership. In many ways these are the necessary antidote for the leader who is tempted to resort to vulnerability in order to establish the rapport he feels he needs.

Jesus Was Prayerful, So He Could Live Genuinely

So often in the life of Christ, we see Him going off alone to pray. He was God, but being fully human, He needed to connect to His Father for strength to live genuinely. His grounding in prayer, which also was coupled with a deep study of the Scripture (which He often quoted), was the foundation for His life. Because He was so spiritually well prepared, Jesus could be genuine at all times.

To see the real nature of someone, you have to look at their actions under pressure or at times when they are surprised and unable to prepare. Going to His torture and death on the cross, Jesus was able to forgive. When awakened from a nap in a boat, He could calm a storm. His life was so completely genuine that there were never times when His character wavered.

Can we say the same thing as leaders? Many of us sign our memos "sincerely," which means genuinely. That is a serious way to frame your signature, because the word *sincere* has its roots in Roman times, when marble cutters began to hide the flaws in the stone they sold by filling in the cracks with wax. And until the weather changed, you couldn't see the cracks. So the Roman government had marble cutters guarantee their stone was not filled with wax by marking it as "sincere." The law didn't require stonecutters to declare their stone was genuine, but the price of saying it was genuine if it was not was execution.

As leaders, we don't have to say we are genuine, but the price of saying we are if we are not is very high. Don't claim Christ if you're not going to live for Him in devotion. It's as simple as that. But genuineness is a process of growing, learning, and always refining and is always changing through the stages and circumstances of life. When we become frustrated by our shortcomings, we need to not live in the frustration of our inadequacy, but instead turn to a deeper walk with God.

Genuineness is an internal measure God gives us to self-evaluate the depth of our relationship with Him. No one else can see even if they describe our outward actions as genuine. When we know in our heart we are lacking in genuineness, this is a time to become more prayerful, go deeper into God's Word, and find the reviving that has come to Christian leaders through the ages. Deepening our walk with Christ produces fruit that allows us to live genuinely, so that in our moments of highest stress or being caught off guard, we reflect the nature of God instead of leaking out our own frustrations in a way that undermines our credibility as leaders.

Jesus Was Confident, So He Could Assure Availability

Jesus was so grounded in His purpose and calling that He could be confident facing an attack, preaching before thousands, or mentoring one Samaritan woman while stopping for a drink. The confidence of Christ wasn't found in the launching of a multi-step master plan to accomplish predetermined objectives. Instead, He lived with the single goal to reveal the nature of God to others, and because He did so, most of the significant ministry moments of Jesus came to Him. Christ had a remarkable way of expressing confidence in His calling by assuring availability. He was available when the sick came … or the critics … or the intellectuals … or the rich … or the poor … or the church leaders … or the worst sinners. His confidence assured His availability.

Studying the daily life of Jesus, we see that most of the people He reached came as interruptions. He was headed one way, and someone came to pull Him another direction. But His confidence was the trigger to know that interruptions were not to be dismissed; rather, they would be His most memorable moments of ministry.

When you are so sure your calling is from God, you can live in confidence, because nothing can keep you from being successful.

Confidence is not about your personality type, developing an aggressive style, or putting on your game face to go out there. Being confident comes from that deep assurance that this is the exact place where God wants you to be, at this exact time, doing this exact thing. Godly confidence burns away the timidity that leads to resorting to vulnerability as a means of gaining approval.

Leaders need to be so sure of their calling to a specific place and time that they can confidently venture into whatever God brings into their path and be thankful for the interruptions that will be their times of most significance. This is part of the basic formula of humility, which elevates the needs of others above our own. (See Phil. 2:3–4.) Leaders who are not being interrupted often—very often—are not doing it right and need to rediscover their calling.

Jesus Was Focused, So He Could Work Purposefully

Jesus lived in this world just as we do, but His focus was toward another place, not this one. He had a perspective that allowed Him to understand what the new heaven and new earth would be, and so His focus was eternal, not earthly. He had been there and would return there, so He had assurance of something that takes lots more trust on our part to grasp. Jesus worked on this earth completely focused toward heaven because He knew it was as genuine as the ground He walked in Galilee.

He prayed to His Father like we would call a loved one to talk about coming home soon from a long trip. To Jesus, heaven and earth were so linked there was no question about heaven's reality. For Him the unseen spiritual world was as absolutely assured as the visible human world. Because of that, Jesus worked purposefully. He prayed, taught, mentored, and loved in ways that connected eternal life with earthly life. He revealed the nature of God that allowed others to see past what is now, and worked purposefully in connection to the world to come.

Jesus handpicked us for leadership and wants us to work as purposefully as He did within the reality of eternity. C. S. Lewis reminds us, "If you read history you will find that the Christians who did most for the present world were just those who thought most of the next…. Aim at Heaven and you will get earth 'thrown in': aim at earth and you will get neither."[7]

Taking the longview is about learning to work with others in light of this eternal perspective. And to be successful we must look to Christ's example and lean on His strength. In doing so we find the depth of love, compassion, humility, and understanding that are the roots of enduring leadership—and in humility we find power to lead as Jesus modeled for us. He washed His disciples' feet, helped them fish, and guided them in their ministry responsibilities. But when Jesus needed to struggle with the vulnerabilities of His humanness, He went alone to His Father, to whom Jesus could even ask, "Could this cup pass?" In His humility—both with those He served unreservedly, and to One He went to in complete transparency during vulnerable moments—Jesus found authentic and lasting power in His leadership.

5

Renewal: The Energy Drink
of Lasting Leadership

Driving through Hollywood headed to a premiere of a new movie, I asked Dr. Ted Baehr, editor of *Movieguide,* a media publication for families of faith, to tell me why Christians have such trouble with the arts. Christians often wince coming near the arts, even when there is so much we could be doing to redeem the arts and influence the media culture in positive ways.

Without hesitation, Ted said, "Christians avoid confrontation rather than seek it out—but the arts are built on conflict." I had never considered that before, but it makes perfect sense. From a sitcom that works out a simple family problem at the end of thirty minutes, to a movie or play that focuses on complex relationships, to a painting that challenges deep thinking, to a symphony that runs from melodic to dissonant, conflict is required for great art.

As followers of Christ we take seriously our call to be peacemakers, and thus we work to minimize personal conflict rather than accentuate it. We can be bold and confident tackling social injustices and moral offenses, but when the conflict moves to a personal level within our own ranks, we prefer to avoid conflict whenever possible. A hard-nosed nonbeliever might not hesitate to use strong language to "tell off" a coworker, and would probably laugh about it later with friends. In contrast, Christian leaders who want to live out their faith have sleepless nights as they prayerfully prepare for the moment when they must deal with the shortcomings of someone else.

As peacemakers, it is appealing to rely on blanket policies that address the whole group rather than directly confront the shortcomings of a few specific individuals. We become convinced that a potential struggle can be minimized following this route. We assume that we must avoid the open wounds of conflict if we are to build unity and harmony within the group.

But the truth is, rather than striving to restrict and control their employees, excellent leaders develop employees through purposefully renewing them. In doing so, these leaders not only find a more substantive and meaningful unity, but also often turn up pure gold in the employees who might otherwise have been considered castoffs. This is the longview model for Christian leaders, and it is thoroughly biblical.

Up Close and Personal

Jesus confronted the disciples individually at times and didn't mince words when He did. He sometimes guided and corrected them as a group, but in the stickiest situations, Jesus went directly to the person and talked straight to him.

In Matthew 16, Jesus was leading the group, and when He sensed one was not on board, He dealt privately with that individual. Only after He confronted the issue Peter raised could Jesus then lead the group to an even deeper understanding of their calling. Follow these three steps as you read the account from Scripture:

> *Jesus began to tell his disciples plainly that it was necessary for him to go to Jerusalem, and that he would suffer many terrible things at the hands of the elders, the leading priests, and the teachers of religious law. He would be killed, but on the third day he would be raised from the dead.*
>
> *But Peter took him aside and began to reprimand him for saying such things. "Heaven forbid, Lord," he said. "This will never happen to you!"*
>
> *Jesus turned to Peter and said, "Get away from me, Satan! You are a dangerous trap to me. You are seeing things merely from a human point of view, not from God's."*
>
> *Then Jesus said to his disciples, "If any of you wants to be my follower, you must turn from your selfish ways, take up your cross, and follow me. If you try to hang on to your life, you will lose it. But if you give up your life for my sake, you will save it." (Matt. 16:21–25)*

Jesus knew what Peter was thinking before He took him aside, and so Christ very easily could have addressed the issue to the whole group—in a policy statement. But instead, He knew that by resolving the conflict head-on with Peter, He would spare the group much confusion, resolve the issue more effectively, and create the climate to call the group to an even higher standard. In addition, looking to the future, Jesus knew His investment in Peter would pay lasting dividends as he took on a critical leadership role in the establishment of the church.

While the leadership example of Jesus seems clear and straightforward, there are at least two ways Christian leaders attempt to circumvent the hard work of developing those they lead: implementing odious policies and searching endlessly for that "perfect" employee. We will examine both of these approaches in turn.

Policies Are for Cowards

Ministries tend to create complex and cumbersome personnel policies in order to become immunized against the small minority of employees who challenge, stretch, or cheat the system, as well as those workers who are by nature difficult people. But these policies don't protect us from confrontation because the very people we seek to avoid are oftentimes the same individuals who are not likely to change without direct correction.

Broad, sweeping policies, which are actually aimed at only a few workers, not only rarely solve the problem, but they slow the grind of the entire ministry by spawning a host of new and more complex issues, draining precious energy from the ministry's mission, and providing irritable employees a framework from which they can legitimately attack the system and hurt the morale of their coworkers.

While employee policies are necessary in every organization, Christian organizations oftentimes are most prone to misuse them. Why is this? Because biblically centered leaders take seriously the command of Jesus in the Sermon on the Mount: "Do not judge others, and you will not be judged…. Why worry about a speck in your friend's eye when you have a log in your own? … Hypocrite!" (Matt. 7:1–5). Those are serious words that should bring us to our knees before carefully dealing with any employee difficulty.

Thus, rather than address a sticky personnel issue head-on, we tend to gravitate toward creating policies (rules) that will "hold us all accountable" without forcing us to specifically judge the actions of one over another. To the same degree that Christians want to avoid judging individuals, we find comfort in absolutes to guide us all. But that option is neither theologically sound nor appropriate when it comes to leadership. We must judge at times, and we can't create one-size-fits-all absolutes to guide us.

For example, all would agree a ministry employee should not spend the better half of the workday signed onto eBay. But rather than dealing directly with the one person in the office who monitors online auctions much of the day, we avoid judging that individual by creating a policy that forbids all employees from any online shopping at any time during work.

With our officewide rule in hand, we are not thrust into the judge's chair to determine how much online shopping is okay, because we have substituted our judgment for an absolute. We may have corrected (temporarily) the behavior of the eBay shopper, but we have frustrated everyone else—and the managers still feel free to punch up Amazon when they come across a new book of interest.

In any good working environment, there will be shades of gray. Exceptions for time schedules, workload, pay scale, and even online shopping will be part of a leader's life. Prayerfully being a good and gracious judge, rather than creating sweeping employee policies, will best solve these personnel issues.

Jesus taught us how to judge, balancing the law with grace. But I find that leaders tend to lean one way over the other rather than find the equilibrium Christ demonstrated. I know many good leaders whose style exhibits a strong bias toward grace and just as many others who operate with a stronger hand on the law. We need both.

As someone who tends to lean toward grace over law, I find in my personnel decisions I especially value my advisors who focus a bit more on the law to help me find the equilibrium Christ modeled for us. This is because evaluation without a standard is ultimately ineffective, just as judgments that don't look past the law are ultimately inadequate, causing us to miss some of our greatest moments for ministry investment in our colleagues.

Our desire to build harmony in the body of Christ is our high calling, but sometimes achieving that end requires us to deal directly with sticky personnel situations. At that time we must not hide sheepishly behind a policy, creating policies to function as surrogate arbitrators, but rather choose to serve as grace-filled judges. This checklist may help you resist the temptation of creating cumbersome employee policies:

1. Does the policy serve your good employees?

Whether the issue is vacation time, expense reports, or hiring procedures, nearly every policy is created in reaction to a very specific problem. That is appropriate, but seeking to prevent a reoccurrence of the same difficulty must not be the only measure of a policy's worth.

Because these policies are created in reaction to an incident with a specific individual, we have that person in mind when we consider the solutions. But before the policy is implemented, also think specifically of some of the good employees to understand how that policy relates to the 96 percent of your team who don't need correction. Think of individual people the policy will impact—go through some of them by name. If it stands up to what is appropriate for your good people, and not just the person who triggered the problem, then it may be a valuable policy to implement.

2. Are those closest to the problem involved in creating the policy?

I've spent too many meetings struggling with health insurance costs because there is no financial pressure that is more significant to my school. Every time we get it tacked down, health insurance finds another way to attack us and impact our bottom line. I've met with all the experts, talked endlessly with my vice presidents, and hammered it through with board members.

Out of fresh ideas from senior leaders, I gave the problem to those who live closest to it, and good things began to happen. We had a breadth of passionate end users serving on a heath insurance task force—a young newlywed, a faculty member nearing retirement, a single parent, an empty nester, and the mother of a family with teenagers. Each came to the problem from a remarkably different perspective.

They educated themselves about insurance and health costs and, in so doing, realized how little most employees know about the issue—so they educated the campus. They focused on wellness rather than sickness and changed the mind-set of many, even offering financial incentives to encourage annual physical exams. They shifted the financial structure to push employees to use generic drugs and adjusted co-pays so that employees discovered the true cost of a doctor's visit.

Not only were the end users more creative in their solutions, but they also became the policy's most important advocates. And every new policy must be stretched and punched by end users if it has any hope of bringing about genuine organizational change.

3. Have you imagined what new problems the policy will create?

Every new policy will trigger a reaction, for good or bad, and a good leader must be able to anticipate issues that could develop if the policy is implemented. Consequences can be severe even when a policy is well intentioned.

I have a college president friend who built a new administration building. To be considerate of donors by saving money, and to demonstrate to the faculty that academic priorities were of higher financial importance, he decided to build the new facility with mostly large, open spaces and planned for all administrators to work in modular offices. It made good sense financially, and the cubicles could easily be reconfigured as the administrative needs changed.

The problem was, the president himself couldn't be in a cubicle because there was just too much confidential talk that went on in his office. And the vice president for finance, who also regularly dealt with sensitive matters, had to be housed in traditional offices in a different building. Others began to build the case for why they also needed privacy. And soon the focus of the corporate culture became stratified between those who could justify walls versus those stuck with no walls. Clearly, this was not the intent of what was a well-meaning policy.

Every potential new-policy decision requires taking the time to project out the possible future ramifications. Leaders should never move ahead with a policy until they have thoroughly envisioned all the possible unintended ramifications of the change.

4. Will you personally live by the policy?

I don't normally look over the shoulder of those in my row when I fly, but the guy in the window seat was too busy to ignore. He was working on his travel expenses, and the heading on his paper made it clear he worked for a large construction company.

It didn't take too long to see his process (since he was spread out on his window-seat tray and the middle-seat tray between us too). He was creating a full-page report for each individual receipt, no matter its size, filling in his name, location where he'd incurred the expense, the purpose of the trip, those present, and a number of other check boxes I couldn't see. And then he would write in the amount—$1.25 for a Pepsi. Then all the same information was handwritten again on a new sheet for the next expense—$16.50 for lunch. It took him the entire flight to complete the financial report for his business trip, and when he totaled it up, it came to less than $300. I couldn't help but imagine how long—and how many people—it must take back in his finance department to process each of those pages as well.

Then I thought of construction-industry leaders I've met. Something tells me this man's boss doesn't spend two hours completing his expense report, but probably puts all his charges on a credit card or just hands his assistant a wad of receipts.

Why should leaders require policies they are not personally willing to live under? They shouldn't, and that is a good benchmark for the value of a policy. If you can't live with it, your people shouldn't either.

The Quest for the Perfect Employee

Just as policies are often more of a liability than a solution, so too your very employees, if not properly developed, can frustrate the leader seeking only to "apply" them as a quick fix to their organization's problems. In the hope of "getting it done right," leaders tend to impose unrealistic assumptions and expectations on their coworkers by using themselves as the consummate measuring rod of perfection.

All of us have seen self-inflated CEOs who find comfort in leadership by surrounding themselves with an army of clones who attempt to act, react, and think in unison. But these leaders never retain good people (if they can attract them in the first place), never free the gifts of all those whom God has brought to the ministry, and never achieve any more than the lowest level of mediocrity for the organization—all the while fooling themselves into believing the ministry is running smoothly because of their efforts to create "perfect employees" who respond to the leader as if they were partners in a three-legged race. Sadly, invariably, such a restrictive approach shrinks the value of all (including the leader) because people are not allowed to be themselves, carry authority, and test their gifts.

An unwillingness to allow coworkers to develop in their unique ways is often driven by a leader's craving to solve immediate problems rather than to make the investment in people that pays off over a longer period of time. But in point of fact, this approach doesn't work for either the short term *or* the long term. Think of encouraging your young child to play the piano—you have to sit through many tedious elementary recitals and pay for years of lessons that seem to be going nowhere before you eventually see the results that make you burst with pride.

Effective ministry leaders make room for the idiosyncrasies, the shortcomings, and even the faults of others, because they know that allowing flexibility among coworkers is the path to creating ownership, commitment, and long-term results. Your responsibility as a leader is to propel the God-given gifts of every employee under your care—even if their way of doing things does not fit the model of what you wish they would be. To do anything less is to squander the rich diversity of gifts, styles, temperaments, and thinking God has given you through your coworkers.

The faulty premise that the leader alone knows the best way to do a job suppresses the productivity of all as they learn to operate out of timidity rather than ingenuity. So you can either embrace the uniqueness of coworkers, freeing them to use their distinctive gifts as God designed, or you can continue to quest after "perfect" employees, trapping them (and you) in an endless cycle of tightening controls, artificial molds, and nuisance policies.

Under Construction

Unlike the laptop we order from Apple, employees don't arrive in our office ready to run flawlessly at top speed right out of the box. Instead, God designed His creations to be developing through a lifelong process of renewal.

Ruth Graham writes, "I once saw a sign on a strip of highway that was under construction. I would like to have that sign copied onto my gravestone. It said, 'End of construction. Thank you for your patience.'"[1] As Ruth reminds us, that process takes a lifetime—because there are no perfect employees (including you and me). But this is one of our highest callings and greatest privileges as leaders—patiently helping our coworkers develop their gifts, vision, and purpose through an ongoing cycle of renewal.

We all need to be people in a process of periodic renewal. Jesus taught that renewal—pruning and growing—is our life blood: "You have already been pruned and purified by the message I have given you. Remain in me, and I will remain in you. For a branch cannot produce fruit if it is severed from the vine, and you cannot be fruitful unless you remain in me" (John 15:3–4).

Building a leadership focus that renews your employees requires careful pruning in order to facilitate new growth. But pruning without giving time and nurture for growth kills the plant, while boundless growth without pruning produces little fruit. Many leaders are eager to correct by pruning, but like the father who doesn't want to turn over the car keys until his teenager has learned to drive perfectly, they never give their employees the chance to experiment, make mistakes, and grow into their success.

Other leaders are anxious to allow their employees the experiences to grow, but they won't deal with the cumbersome work of pruning to help them use their 20/20 hindsight and the perspective of others to understand the process of their growth and become their own best critics.

Once, while working with one of those ministries that never fires anyone because everyone is somehow interconnected, I inherited an employee who had aggravated many of the others in the organization because he didn't fit the mold. He was a big, burly guy who was passionate about the mission and had a heart of gold. He had been tried in a variety of jobs to find the right fit, and none seemed to work out right. Different managers had tried a multitude of methods to make him conform, resulting in only minimal behavioral changes to show for their struggle.

What I found was that no one had seemed to focus on both the growth and the pruning. Through a dialogue identifying his calling and gifts, we laid out together a plan for a job that was creative, interesting, and challenging. Then we built around the job description measures of success, operational boundaries, and checkpoints for shooting straight with each other to fine-tune our approach.

Although many in the organization never understood why I allowed him to come into the office after lunch to begin his day, they were thrilled with the results that he produced as he worked until midnight or later. He never wore a blue suit that made him look the consummate professional, but his genuine relationships with people who didn't even own suits raised a ton of money for us. And his inability to create a systematic operational plan was insignificant in comparison to his ability to recruit enthusiastic volunteers who could carry the load.

The employee others wanted to discard was far from a "perfect employee," but he was one of my favorites as I watched him grow and be pruned to become one of the go-to people in the organization.

Renewal for the Longview

As Christian leaders, we desire to be used of God to reach scores of people for Christ, build programs and facilities that are lasting, and infuse our sphere of influence with biblical ideas—but there is nothing farther reaching and more lasting than the renewal of our employees. As they become more fruitful through the process of pruning and growing, God graciously allows our reach to extend far beyond ourselves. But you will not ignite renewal in those who work with you if you are not first committed to your own personal journey of renewal.

For yourself and your team, you need to learn to create a culture of renewal that is (1) dramatic, (2) deliberate, and (3) discerning.

1. Learning from the dramatic moments triggers renewal.

New Year's resolutions don't cause many people to eat right and exercise long term, but a heart-attack scare will do it almost every time. Any life-pattern adjustment that moves far beyond teeth-gritting determination is usually born out of a dramatic moment.

Those dramatic moments are more often negative than positive, but we can have assurance in the sovereignty of God that He is using the hard times to teach and prepare us for what is yet to come. When life comes against us, we need to be looking to where God wants to push us rather than only pushing back.

A student emailed me just before graduation to tell me how her world had fallen apart during the final semester of her education. She was a marvelous student that I'd watched overcome challenges of home and school early in her career, and I had enjoyed seeing her grow in grace. But during that last term, one thing on top of another seemed to turn against her, and to top it off, what she believed was an unfair low grade from her professor kept her from receiving the graduation honors she probably deserved.

Of course, only days before commencement, there was little to do to change the circumstances, and so in my email response I encouraged her to look with anticipation for why God had allowed these challenges—

Dear Sarah,

I'm sorry you've had this difficulty here at the end of your college journey. I've often prayed for you, knowing you've had to overcome the tough obstacles that we've talked about in the past. But even in this last setback, God will use it all for His glory.

For some reason, the Lord is preparing you to take on something very difficult and significant for the future, and He knows the only way to get you ready is for you to have these challenges now. What is it? Keep asking and preparing because it will be worth the struggle. I'll be anxious to watch your life to see how God is going to use you.

And about the honors: God gives the honors that matter, and being right in His eyes is much more important than any honors we can give you as a college.

RP

Painful experiences that require choosing between rejection or renewal bring about changes that become seared in our emotional memory—we can all remember a difficult lesson learned in junior high as vividly as if it happened yesterday. But renewing experiences don't always need to be negative. And in orchestrating teachable experiences, leaders need to craft challenges that bring about lasting renewal. Adding responsibilities, broadening the scope of supervision, or even celebrating accomplishments will become dramatic events that trigger direction-changing renewal in the lives of employees.

Oftentimes the gigantic shifts in our lives, organizations, and society begin with a small moment of drama. Those who are renewed look for the unsettledness that can be the seedbed of change. Sometimes the trigger comes into our life because the Lord is testing and preparing us for something. Other times the stress comes because we've made bad choices and there are consequences to our actions. And hopefully, renewal is ignited because of the opportunities provided by insightful leaders. But no matter the source, God will use the dramatic moments to launch us into renewal if we are willing.

2. Deliberate action energizes renewal.

While the dramatic moments of opportunity or disappointment may trigger renewal, the real work is carried out in careful day-to-day follow-through. Without ongoing implementation, our desire for renewal is fairly empty.

Renewal is not a one-time event. Like the life of holiness, renewal begins with a commitment, but then we must deepen, grow, and recommit ourselves continually to God's calling. And in that process of sanctification, we can live and work confidently. Living in the center of God's will is not a destination as much as it is a journey.

If we are going to be people who are renewed, sometimes it is best to just do something, even if it is not the ultimate change that needs to be made. To get renewal moving, you need to look both inside and outside your normal job responsibilities, so maybe the best thing you could do for your ministry is to ...

- Take a day to see your ministry from a bird's-eye view rather than focus only on your own area of responsibility.
- Put the same level of energy into loving your kids and your spouse that you put into your job.
- Get back into a routine of daily devotions.
- Make a list of ways you can work smarter.

- Take the time to fix something you'll never get credit for doing.
- Read something new in your field or, if you can stand it, outside your field.
- Pray specifically for the people with whom you most closely work.

Some action, even if it doesn't focus on the area needing attention, can trigger renewal in other arenas. While a well-developed plan of renewal would seem admirable, I've found that just keeping the ball rolling is sometimes the key to grooving a path for change.

3. Discerning relationships accelerates renewal.

To develop a culture of renewal, you must become comfortable living with the ambiguous balance of growth and pruning in your working relationships. Change in people will come with a grind of starts and stops, ups and downs, surprises and embarrassments.

Renewal is never easy. It is complex and messy, and only in hindsight is it usually attractive and admired. It is not the comfortable route for us or for those we are helping to renew. But our calling demands a commitment to the disruptive work of renewal if we are to utilize fully the gifts of the people God has brought to us.

I once knew a remarkable college president who was nearing retirement after a stellar career. Even though he was physically suffering from the wear of the years, he came to the job every day with a commitment to release the gifts of the people around him. He took under his wing a twenty-six-year-old new PhD who had not been tested or seasoned. The president put this young man into situations that sometimes worked out great—and other times he had to clean up the mess his protégé had made. He entrusted the young man with far more responsibility than anyone should have at that age, and the president never backed up when he was criticized for doing so.

Nearly daily, he was growing and pruning the one he may have seen as a younger version of himself. He would teach from the moments of drama, provide assurance in the ongoing process of growth, and prune when the door was shut, so corrections could be made in private rather than with embarrassment. And don't think he ever stopped praying for the one he was mentoring.

I've often thought how much easier it would have been for that president to go out and hire a top-quality administrator who had already been through the fires and could carry the responsibility with ease and grace during the final years of his presidency. But I'm sure glad he didn't, or I never would have had the chance to grow and be pruned for much more to come since my years with Dr. Curt Smith.

It would be orderly for us as leaders to go out and attempt to hire "perfect employees" who fit our needs for the moment. But we will have missed our calling in leadership if we run from the disruptions necessary to allow every employee the opportunity to grow and be pruned to become all God intends. Renewal in their lives—and ours—will not be an efficient straight line of progress. But when we respond to the call of leadership, renewal is a solid line of God's strength and God's outcome.

Christ-Honoring Leadership

Jesus had no perfect disciples, just as we find that we have no "perfect employees." But when we work to create an expectation of renewal for ourselves and for the entire team under our care, it is remarkable how well employees will rise to the call—because God made us to be people who crave renewal. He made us to need renewal in order to be productive, creative, and happy. Likewise, God made us to respond much more readily to a personable and gracious pruning rather than to a set of detached, rigid policies.

Whether founded in passion and vision or hurt and desperation, renewal is in the fabric of our relationship with God—and facilitating Christ-honoring renewal is our highest responsibility in leadership. Our objective must never be to manipulate those we serve into our image, but rather to help prune and grow them into the image of Christ. Leaders who solve their problems with one employee after another or one policy on top of another, instead of making the investment in people that pays off over a longer period of time, will never reach the significance found in longview leadership. And they will stifle rather than release the gift each individual can be to their organization.

Jesus gently guided, directly corrected, and insightfully taught a rough-edged, burly young man who too often responded with lashing emotion rather than measured reason—and then gave him ample space to allow him to learn and grow. And in doing so, He pruned and grew Peter into one He called "the Rock," on which Christ could build His church.

6

The Bookends of a Leader's Character: Evaluation and Accountability

One snowy day in Kansas, I fired a professor for unethical conduct. I watched out my office window as he headed to his car, knowing his life would never be the same again. He had to go home to tell his wife what happened, somehow justify his breach of ethics to her—and find ways to blame the college in the process. He had to explain to his kids why he was not going to work the next day, and why their birthdays would be leaner this year, and why they would need to move soon and leave their school friends behind. He would need to break the news to his parents, proud of their professor son, and share it with a host of friends who would speculate behind his back about what "really happened." And that didn't begin to count the difficulty he would face trying to explain the situation to prospective employers.

The logistical and relationship challenges of being fired are only the tip of the iceberg compared to the complex emotional turmoil it creates. Being fired is not just losing a paycheck: It thrusts one into an agonizing pit of questions regarding self-worth, calling, and future—not the least of which is, "Why did God let this happen to me?"

Donald Trump may earn millions by firing someone publicly, but when I watched that crushed faculty member walk from my office, I just wanted to cry—even though he brought the dismissal on himself.

I have fired many people through the years, but I don't like it and don't do it lightly. Firing someone must be a last resort, but there are times when, for the good of the ministry, we must fire an employee. And we also have to trust God that in firing someone, it will be the best for the employee as well. A termination is the conclusion of an evaluative process followed up by accountability, designed for the renewal of the employee. It is oftentimes the fullest expression of the longview, bearing the future of all concerned in mind.

Tools of the Trade

Medieval Catholic monk and author of *The Imitation of Christ* Thomas à Kempis wrote, "Be not angry that you cannot make others as you want them to be, since you cannot make yourself as you wish to be." As a leader, you can't make anyone else change, but we do have tools at our disposal to help us bring those we serve further along.

In chapter 5 we touched on the importance of pruning in developing employees. This is critical to their renewal, which is our highest goal for them. Now we turn the page to look at the two primary tools used to accomplish this work: evaluation and accountability. Evaluation is a precision tool, used for sharpening and defining. Accountability is the backbone of evaluation, providing a foundation on which to build and reinforce excellence at every level of your organization. Leaders who neglect effective evaluation and measured accountability may avoid short-term hassles and awkward conversations, but they are undermining the long-term future of their organization, their employees, and their own leadership.

Evaluation Releases the Pressure Valve

I both love and hate evaluations, but I know a ministry cannot be effective without doing them right. The wisdom of Proverbs should be the music in our ears as we keep evaluation a priority in our ministries:

> *People who accept discipline are on the pathway to life, but those who ignore correction will go astray. (10:17)*

> *To learn, you must love discipline; it is stupid to hate correction. (12:1)*

> *If you reject discipline, you only harm yourself; but if you listen to correction, you grow in understanding. (15:32)*

But despite these scriptural injunctions, employee evaluations may be the most mishandled arena of leadership, even in Christian organizations. And yet, if done well and in the right spirit, evaluation can be the most helpful tool of leadership.

Too often evaluation is a *hammer* waiting to fall … a *feather* floating away … a *shadow* following behind.

Each of those poor alternatives leads to complexities that eventually impair quality relationships, prevent meaningful accountability, and stifle an enriching ministry culture.

The Hammer Evaluation

Tom DeLay was known as "The Hammer" when he served as majority whip in the House of Representatives because he could force members to vote how the party leadership wished. He didn't do that through his power of persuasion, but through a deliberate system of rewards and punishments. If you voted as desired, you were given the best committee assignments and opportunities for media attention, and your ideas were considered for future legislation. If you didn't, all that could (and would) be taken away until an elected member's role became insignificant.

In organizations where heavy-handed annual evaluations are used to threaten or control employees, the effects are likewise detrimental. Not only is the level of anxiety raised by the evaluation's dominance, but just like students who focus only on "what is on the test" rather than mastering the material, employees soon learn to work in ways that will shape the outcome of their evaluations. Further, employees tend to build their tasks around comfortable evaluation periods so that they always appear in control of the work under scrutiny, instead of pushing a schedule faster or slower as the job demands. They avoid taking risks or stretching themselves, and in turn stifle creativity and suppress innovation for fear of a poor review.

Another unintended consequence of a controlling evaluation culture is that power differentials are created among those who should be pulling together as work-team members. Everyone becomes more focused on the eventual evaluation than on the task at hand. If a group is to work essentially as peers until that magic moment when the review dramatically elevates one member over the others, it becomes a dysfunctional and ineffective unit.

Within any ministry it is certainly appropriate to create pressure, expectations, and demands for quality. We are all more productive with deadlines and standards of excellence to steer us. But when that pressure is focused primarily on the evaluation—and in most organizations like this the hammer evaluation seems to be the only tool used to create intensity—it is ineffective, discouraging, and depleting.

The Feather Evaluation

I was not surprised to listen to the groans of a third-level director of a major denomination talking about needing to get his evaluations completed; evaluation is not intrinsically a comfortable process. But without even knowing the prescribed structure, I could tell from his tone that the evaluation was not viewed as an opportunity to improve his team. Rather, the evaluation was something to check off the to-do list in order to feed the system and avoid triggering difficulties for himself and his people in the process. And I'm sure that as he went through the motions of a feather-touch evaluation, it didn't make one bit of difference to anyone.

A top-to-bottom evaluation requirement is an important policy for every ministry to maintain, and the flaws of the system should not keep you from prioritizing it. Any mechanism demanding an evaluation number for each item in a preset list of criteria will substitute artificial scoring for meaningful outcomes. By requiring a supervisor to fill out grades (usually one to five) like the left side of a first grader's report card (e.g., "plays well in groups"), this type of evaluation creates a manufactured context in which the "score" becomes more important than discussion of genuine improvement. In most ministries where this is required, "grade inflation" has taken over so that nearly everyone gets a five on all scores, except for one or two measures—because the evaluation policy makes it clear no one is allowed to have a perfect score.

Another flaw in any evaluation system is failure to vary the criteria and procedures based on the position of the employee. This broad-brush approach devalues the entire exercise. How can you use the same criteria for a custodian and a CEO? (I've seen that in ministries.) Or how can you use the same criteria on two people doing the same job when one is new in the profession and the other has been at it for twenty years? (Equal performance should not be good enough.) If the criteria are broad enough to fit everyone, you limit the evaluation to the lowest common denominator of the entire group.

Just as you cannot simply normalize the criteria for all, neither can an effective system normalize the rewards for success. Effective evaluation should produce something to change, something to celebrate, something to learn, and something to earn. And while money is not a primary motivator in ministry, it is amazing to me how often ministries will favor across-the-board increases with minimal differences between those who bring the most value-added and those who are just filling a seat. If evaluation matters, then the salary should show it.

On final analysis, a feather-light structure can create a false sense of success because the evaluation does not address issues that help employees to grow and become stronger—and for the least effective people, it cements their pattern of minimal effort. To mentor people, you must share ways in which they could do a better job; any less is to squander the talents of those whom God has entrusted to you and create a culture of entrenched mediocrity.

The Shadow Evaluation

Robert Louis Stevenson wrote:

> I have a little shadow that goes in and out with me,
> And what can be the use of him is more than I can see.

An unused evaluation process is a lot like a shadow—hovering in the background and serving no meaningful purpose.

A board chair once told me, proudly, "We don't need to evaluate our president; things have never been better since he came a few years ago." He went on to explain how the board had a process in place if "we ever need it," but since things were going so well, they saw no need to "muddy the waters with evaluation." A couple years later, that same president was fired.

Too many ministries think in terms of having an evaluation only when they need it, and that is too late. If a CEO goes for years without an evaluation, and then the board calls for one, the problem has already grown to such a difficult stage that just announcing an evaluation is itself the verdict. Certainly, when all seems well, it is tempting to shelve the evaluation process for the best employees. Often there is little to correct, and/or it is difficult to set aside time for an evaluation when it is assumed little will come of it. Moreover, supportive boards or administrators don't want their top people to feel threatened by the process.

But I would argue that, especially when things are going well for you, there is nothing more important than an evaluation. And although skipping the exercise might be comfortable in the short term, doing so will hurt you in the long run; so insist upon being evaluated annually in a structured way. No matter your position, if you're not now being evaluated, you need to initiate the process rather than wait for it to come to you. Boards who oversee highly successful CEOs may still be tempted to avoid evaluation, but savvy executives demand annual evaluation because they find ways to make the exercise helpful for themselves and the ministry.

Four Cornerstones of Evaluation

The following four-point justification for a meaningful evaluation is directed at CEOs because the standard must start at the top, but the same principles work for those outside the corner office as they work with their superiors:

1. Scheduled evaluation releases the pressure valve.

Any leader who has served for a time will have detractors; hard decisions and management style conflicts can rub more painfully over time. Like a car with a radiator prone to overheating, periodically releasing the pressure valve through evaluation will keep issues from building up. For this reason, I never hold a board meeting without an executive session with the CEO in attendance, followed by a continued executive session without the CEO.

2. Evaluation provides a contained framework for negative talk.

Especially within boards, there are always a few members who feel they are fulfilling their responsibility only when they find some fault with the CEO. But if they have no outlet for their criticisms, their talk can cause significant damage as it leaks out in other venues.

3. Evaluation shows you're not chicken.

If I could see into the private thoughts of CEOs, I am convinced I'd see the reason they tolerate empty evaluation policies throughout their ministry is that they want to avoid evaluation themselves. When one of my wisest mentors, Dr. Tom Zimmerman, who served twenty-six years as general superintendent of the Assemblies of God, initiated an evaluation process for the entire denomination, he started with the board evaluating him.

4. Evaluation allows you to celebrate the match.

If you're a good leader, there will not be a laundry list of recommendations coming out of an evaluation. So use this as a time to celebrate that God has brought together the right leader, for the right ministry, at the right time. When the match of leader and ministry fits, it is only because God knows what we will become, not just who we are. Good leaders are no longer directing the same ministry to which they were called—yes, the organization's name and location are the same, but both the leader and ministry have matured, and you need times to celebrate that the match is still right.

An Evaluation Model That Works

Not having a scheduled evaluation creates a dam into which little issues begin to collect until eventually they impact the flow of the river. To break that logjam with dynamite all at once can significantly harm a relationship and a leader's effectiveness. In contrast, when evaluation is a systematic process, the smaller issues are addressed before they become barriers, and the pressure is never allowed to build.

I have test-driven about every evaluation system that has come through *Harvard Business Review* since its founding in 1922, and I have hated most of them. While I wouldn't begin to prescribe one evaluation system that meets the needs of every organization (because culture, history, and personalities are important in finding the right fit), there are five characteristics that should be evident in any evaluation system:

Flexible

One size does not fit all evaluators, any more than it fits all those being evaluated. Good leaders know you can't motivate two people in the exact same way, so don't attempt to evaluate them with an ironclad system either. Additionally, managers each have their own style with their work groups, and if you impose an organizationwide structured evaluation system on a relational manager, it will be as phony as requiring a conversational review for a button-down manager.

Layered

An annual review is probably the most convenient structure around which to build a formal evaluation, but once a year is not often enough. Too much can change in a year. Thus, to have a layered evaluation structure that includes a less formal insight exchange quarterly (or at some other natural stopping point) can enable issues of concern to be discussed with fresh and meaningful reflection. In my setting at a college, I focus on three key times, built around the natural breaks in the year—structured comfortably at the start of each semester and the beginning of summer.

Deliberate

The only time my dear mother still thinks of me as a fifteen-year-old teenager is when I get behind the wheel of her car. I get more correction in the first mile than I get all the rest of my driving year. Ironically, however, when she rides with me, I find it doesn't make me a better driver, but rather one that is more cautious and prone to error, because I'm on edge waiting for the next time her foot will come down on her imaginary brake pedal. And evaluation is the same way. Constant evaluation makes for jumpy workers, not better ones—thus the times of evaluation need to be deliberate.

Convergent

Evaluations have not taken full advantage of the moment if the discussion never turns the table to ask how the ministry, the boss, and the other team members can be more helpful to the one being evaluated. This two-way look can be a wonderful time of strengthening for both sides, helping each to fulfill their shared mission more effectively.

Actionable

The majority of any review is likely to be positive, but as issues demanding attention are addressed, they need to be presented specifically and accompanied by benchmarks for change. Don't assume that your employees are doing something poorly on purpose. Maybe they have never been taught a different way, or perhaps they are so wrapped up in their tasks they don't realize the damage caused by their attitude. There is no fairness in pointing out faults without also pointing the way to solutions. When dealing with an especially negative review, growth plans need to be formally written together, and a date set for the follow-up review. Unless agreement can be reached regarding the issues of concern, no change is likely to come, so buy in from the one being reviewed is critical.

Lofty

At the end of the day, the review system must build up the organization and its people, not tear them down. An employee may have earned emotion-laden, harsh correction, but as leaders whose responsibility is to renew those in our care, delivering cutting "constructive criticism" is not the end objective of evaluation. Rather it is bringing about "constructive change" that must remain our lofty goal, and we must suppress any vengeful words that could keep us from our ultimate goal.

"You're Accountable!"

A meaningful evaluation is an actionable one that leads to renewed goals, change, and vigor. But it goes hand in hand with accountability, which is the ongoing support structure that is strengthened through the periodic event of evaluation. Each of us achieves God's best when we embrace the accountability structure that surrounds us rather than seeking to circumvent it.

It is unhealthy for ministry climate, productivity, and relationships if employees feel they do not need to be ultimately accountable. God designed us to be accountable to Him through the people He has brought into our lives—spouse, children, supervisor, coworkers, and those we serve.

Accountability does not just run down the organizational chart, but spreads across it in all directions as well. Accountability is not simply one person holding power over another. Done right, accountability—not unlike evaluation—is always reciprocal, driven by an "iron sharpens iron" vision of working relationships. While employees may have more formal accountability to supervisors, the responsibility downward on the organizational structure should not be any less. The ministry workplace must be a covenant relationship of accountability in which informal accountability trumps hierarchy.

Even boards are accountable to those they serve and to the CEO who works with them, rather than operating in autonomy.

When I moved from vice president to president in the college ranks, I assumed that the job would come with less accountability than what I had always shouldered serving a president who demanded much and wanted it quickly. But nothing could be further from the truth, because the CEO job has accountability folded into it at every layer. The formal accountability of the board is critical, but I am aware every day of the accountability I have to do a good job for those under my care and am rightfully more aware of my accountability to them than I am to "my boss," the board. This is how it should be, because if a CEO feels only accountable to the board, the leader will create inappropriate power differentials, will fail to build teamwork or shared mission, and will be short-lived in usefulness to the ministry.

Getting the best from accountability is more about an attitude than a function; it boils down to our *desire* to be accountable. If employees only stubbornly accept the insights of their supervisor or coworkers, they dramatically limit their effectiveness. At the same time, supervisors who use accountability as a weapon of control rather than a brace of support miss the value it can bring to the office. Some in leadership hold over employees an ongoing awareness of the termination possibility or make demands on them that demonstrate how little they trust them. That iron grip is not accountability at all but the mark of an insecure boss.

Proper accountability finds balance in our employee relationships—too much is stifling, and too little is deadly. We need to find that center point that helps everyone to stretch, grow, and perform best. Without accountability, we all tend to drift toward mediocrity in our performance, and too often, sinful nature takes advantage of gaps in accountability—ministry leaders fall for many different reasons, but they all have in common a lack of accountability in their lives. Arch Hart of the Fuller Seminary faculty captures it well: "Accountability to another is the only way to safeguard against poor judgment, unconscious motivations, and self-deception."[1]

God designed us to be people of accountability, and some of the Bible's strongest warnings are related to a life without accountability.

Both the Old and New Testaments make it plain: "Remember that you must give an account to God for everything you do" (Eccl. 11:9); "Yes, each of us will give a personal account to God" (Rom. 14:12).

Jesus said, "A good person produces good things from the treasury of a good heart, and an evil person produces evil things from the treasury of an evil heart. And I tell you this, you must give an account on judgment day for every idle word you speak" (Matt. 12:35–36).

Isaiah 47:10–11 assures catastrophe to those who say, "I am the only one, and there is no other."

The message of the parable of the talents is accountability of our gifts: "After a long time their master returned from his trip and called them to give an account of how they had used his money" (Matt. 25:19).

The Bible details the level of accountability expected from us in the workplace through the example of work situations involving an abusive boss: "Slaves, obey your earthly masters in everything you do. Try to please them all the time, not just when they are watching you. Serve them sincerely because of your reverent fear of the Lord" (Col. 3:22).

In other words, if you're not willing to be accountable because you don't have the perfect boss, that excuse doesn't hold up in the eyes of God. If accountability is important for a slave, then it is central for all of us in our working life.

Accountability is laced into nearly every relationship throughout the Bible. Jesus picked twelve disciples because He knew they would need accountability to each other after He was gone. Paul the older mentor, Barnabas the unvarnished peer, and Timothy the young apprentice did not always see eye to eye, but together they made each other stronger. David experienced leadership with and then without accountability, and was anxious to return to the restoration and balance he found in the former. Noah needed the family accountability system of his three sons to help him build the ark.

We all need accountability, even though we may not always like it and sometimes scheme to avoid it. The consequences of living without accountability are too destructive:

> We could not bear to live in a world where wrong is taken
> lightly, where right and wrong finally make no difference....
> Spare me a gospel of easy love that makes of my life a thing
> without consequence.... Atonement is not an accountant's
> trick. It is not a kindly overlooking; it is not a not counting

> of what must count if anything in heaven or on earth is to
> matter. God could not simply decide not to count without
> declaring that we do not count.[2]

We need each other to make God's plan of accountability work. "Walk with the wise and become wise; associate with fools and get in trouble" (Prov. 13:20). Anyone who comes to work and is not held accountable is working counter to God's design and becomes a drain on the entire group.

The Untouchables

Unfortunately, ministries have become sprinkled with too many who feel they are above accountability. Maybe because they raise their personal support, or allow calling to trump work ethic, or view full-time ministry as being responsible only to God rather than God's people, their patterns create a significant problem in ministries. Leaders must learn never to hire those they can't fire, and in turn, create a culture of accountability for all.

"Untouchables" in the ministry workplace are people who feel they don't have to be held accountable in the same way as others. These are not bad people; in fact, many of them may have been hired because they are, in fact, exceptional individuals. But while their motives may be pure, their attitudes and actions put a strain on everyone in the ministry.

These employees who feel they can live above accountability demands normally come to our employment from any one of a variety of connections to the organization. Perhaps they are relatives of another employee or close friends with an employee from another context, such as a church. Or perhaps they are one of those exceptionally gifted people whose second-to-none talents brought them into the organization somewhat abruptly, no questions asked. And of course there are always some who have been with the ministry long enough to feel they have "earned the right" to do what they want to do in the way they want to do it, and are accountable only to themselves.

Such people somehow believe they are protected against being held to the same standard of accountability as everyone else. They may show they are "untouchable" in many ways:

- Ignoring the process of expense report audits or other administrative mechanisms
- Purposefully keeping different hours from the rest of the office
- Holding possessively to their projects, donors, or travel plans
- Cutting corners, working leisurely, or appearing uncaring about outcomes
- Turning a blind eye to needs outside the small domain they control
- Reminding their supervisor of information they know that could be damaging
- Dropping periodic hints about legal challenges they could bring against the ministry
- Doing what they prefer to do, rather than what they are needed to do

These issues become more complex because the influence of these people goes far beyond their own responsibilities and tensions with a supervisor. Ranging from annoyance to obstruction, their independence impedes the entire workflow. These untouchables tend to trigger jealousy, frustration, and discontent in others, becoming the topic of much watercooler talk. Eventually the office learns to "work around them" to achieve the group goals.

Two measures are accurate barometers to gauge whether you are dealing with untouchable people. First, if they quit tomorrow, would you be relieved? Second, are you inordinately cautious working with them because of a relationship they have outside the normal structure of the organizational chart? If you answer a resounding yes to either question, you need to do the hard work of building accountability into their expectations, or let them go. If your answer is a meek yes, you may be able to live with them—for now.

All untouchable employees come with a set of challenges. Each must be addressed prayerfully, graciously, and patiently. Avoiding these types of employees altogether is not the solution for ministry leadership, because they describe so many in our employment pool. But we need to go into these situations with our eyes open, making sure these challenging relationships have the right foundation and structure built into them so that immunity from accountability does not settle in.

Five Tension-Relieving Steps

A leader is never likely to curtail completely the freedom felt by employees who believe themselves less accountable because of other relationships. If the board chair's son works for you, nothing can change the fact that he'll always be the board chair's son. But leaders can relieve some of the tension in working with employees who pose special challenges of accountability. While these are easy steps to recommend—and extremely difficult to implement—the option of not taking action is even more painful for the ministry, the leader, the cause of Christ, and as Scripture tells us, even for the employees themselves.

Get a Fresh Start

The tension a leader feels with an employee who operates beyond accountability will never be solved through gentle nudges. A purposeful discussion (not one in the hallway) is needed to deal with these issues forthrightly. The agenda for the meeting might include a discussion that begins as follows:

> We need to talk about the potential problems I see developing because your wife is one of our vice presidents. We value the gifts you bring to us, and being her husband shouldn't limit what we do, but I'd like to be candid about the ways I'm seeing this relationship hamper our working together effectively.

This fresh-start discussion most often needs to happen with the employee, but you may need to have the same discussion with his vice-president wife. Or, if you are the one who has the connection-skewed relationship, you should be the one to initiate the conversation with your supervisor.

Don't Stop Being the Leader

In ministry, our personal lives and our work lives tend to overlap. That can be a wonderful thing on many levels, but if left unchecked, it can hinder accountability when leaders attempt to turn off their responsibility.

Leaders must be consistent if nothing else. To be your coworkers' buddy in one setting and their boss in another is disconcerting unless you purposefully separate the two. If you go to church with employees on Sunday, it is not possible to be "one of the boys" joking in the narthex and to hold very firmly to the mantle of leadership the rest of the week. A bit of distance is important for healthy leadership, and that cannot be turned off and on with a switch.

Schedule Time for Friendship

If you go to Sunday school with your coworker, it is easy for the small-group prayer time to become a budget meeting. If your kids are on the same Little League team as the children of your administrative assistant, it is a challenge not to take the office to the ballpark, too. If you take family vacations with a fellow vice president, it is tough for the trip not to become a planning retreat. The only way to deal with these situations is to schedule deliberate breaks between your work and personal lives.

At the same time, a wonderful agreement to make with donors who began as friends outside the context of your ministry is to have a deliberate distinction between work and friendship. Any potential tension with your friend/donor can be broken by sched-uling specific times during the year to talk business—with the understanding that the rest of the time is designated for friendship alone. Thus at the appointed times you can ask for a gift and lay out the ministry needs, but the rest of the time, you're free to relate as friends without any other expectations.

Exaggerate the Accountability Plan

As soon as the office knows that the newly hired director is the daughter of the founding president, everyone will be suspicious of her, no matter how well she performs on the job. When employees with extenuating relationships are among us, their errors are magnified, the scrutiny is heightened, and coworkers are slow to trust the new person.

It may help to allay suspicions surrounding both the employee and those who hire and/or supervise her, if the accountability plan for that person is deliberately accentuated—and both the leader and the new employee work together to do so. When oth-ers see the founder's daughter filling out an expense report with the same detail they are required to have, tensions are dimin-ished. When it is demonstrated that her workload is as heavy as it was for the person she replaced, misgivings are abated. When occasions are found to let others gently know she is not receiving special privileges or information, jealousies are assuaged. Over time, the nepotistic employee can be accepted the same as others, but visually exaggerating the accountability plan can accelerate that process.

Hire Them on Purpose

Each time we hire a new employee with baggage, we are convinced "this time will be different." We tell ourselves the issues we've had with others whom we could not fire will not apply to this person. But more often than not, we will face difficulties leading people who have unique relationships to others in our ministry, and dealing with those questions up front can go a long way toward avoiding severe problems down the road.

One of my donors pushed me hard to hire his daughter as a coach. She was a wonderful woman and talented in many ways. And so I asked her father, "Will we still be friends, and will you still be a strong supporter if it doesn't work out and I have to fire her someday?" He assured me it would be impossible for his daughter's working with us to harm his commitment to our school or to me. But once she got on the job, she felt she didn't need to put the effort into the job like others, and so did the parts of the work she enjoyed and let the rest go. After two years, we couldn't take it any longer, and despite multiple accountability plans for corrective action, we fired her. My donor sent me a hot letter to tell me why we were totally wrong and his daughter was totally right. He's never spoken to me since, and we've not seen another gift. I too thought this time would be different, but it never is unless corrective steps are taken up front.

Wise and insightful leaders can learn to work with these special employees. But it will take a careful and purposeful plan to help them fulfill the Lord's best in the ministry and for all employees to accept the uniquely connected employee as a welcome addition rather than a focal point of frustration.

What If You Do Nothing?

The long-term consequences of a life without correction and accountability are staggering. Neglecting effective evaluation may momentarily feel like escaping a checkup with the dentist, but over time, a mouthful of root-canal work will be much more painful that the preventive visit. Accountability to a board, boss, spouse, coworkers, and even your children is God's gift to each of us to assure we strive for lasting quality in our lives.

If Christians will reposition evaluation and accountability for what they genuinely are, we can embrace them as godly tools for becoming all that the Lord desires for us. Without these two bookends to hold us upright we are destined for a life of tragedy, failure, and mediocrity—which may come later than sooner, but it will come.

7

Preempting the Stickiest Challenge of Long-Term Leadership

The powerful gravitational pull of a new ministry's compelling vision brought together a committed handful of wealthy friends who wanted to free their funds from the limits of bureaucratic organizational structures in order to achieve their laser-focused ministry objectives on the ground. They allowed around their table only those who shared their passion, wealth, and urgency for results, and because they didn't have to conform to a preset ministry pattern, they were on an exceptionally fast growth track as they launched the venture.

Within this group, the two largest donors each had a capable young son, about the same age, who had developed equally strong leadership gifts, zeal, and drive. The full board agreed the tandem was ideal to direct this effort—each with equal title, responsibility, and salary—both reporting directly to the board. One young leader carried the task of developing the resources, while the other implemented the work around the world.

Going into the dual leader arrangement, the board acknowledged the potential conflict of interest with their parents as board members and major donors, but they knew they were all well-intentioned, good people, and thus moved ahead with the expectation they could avoid pitfalls. But within just a few weeks after the launch, each hard-driving, successful father became aggressive in directing his own son—and then, finding fault with the other. Within a year, the board became divided as each father used the promise of gifts, or the threat of withholding support, to get his own son preference. Inordinate energy at all levels was given to dealing with the personal tension rather than the passion that first brought them together—the potential conflict of interest had become one.

Within two years, several board members dropped out rather than address the struggle; giving and ministry opportunities had leveled off and staff was reduced; board meetings became a framework for the feud, rather than envisioning what God might do through them. In disgust, one father quit, the other son resigned—and then, uncomfortably for all, the second father resigned as well, making room for the first father of the one still employed to return to the board. Needless to say, the ministry never came close to achieving its potential, and relationships were irreparably damaged.

Managing the tensions and avoiding difficulties by using evaluation and accountability among employees is the little league of leadership compared to the insight and finesse necessary to handle the complexity of conflicts of interest that are likely to arise in any ministry. From both inside and outside the organization there will be those who, knowingly or unknowingly, seek to personally benefit, improperly influence, or somehow manipulate your organization and in doing so create a tangled conflict of interest. If left unchecked, it is rarely a matter of *if,* but usually only a matter of *when,* before a potential conflict of interest takes root and becomes a significant problem.

Conflicts of interest can be found in board relationships, business incentives, employee situations, or scores of other corners of a ministry. Effective leaders must hold fast to a longview perspective as conflicts begin to bubble up, looking to take early action in order to preempt a long-term catastrophe that will possibly limit ministry options.

Even though it may take months or possibly years for the troubling potential to evolve into tension, longview leaders understand that a potential conflict of interest will always become one if left unaddressed. While most moderately experienced leaders can identify a rising conflict-of-interest situation, few take the action to manage the potential problem at the outset and wait until the difficulty has bloomed rather than nip it in the bud.

Diagnostic Triggers

Some conflicts of interest can be seen a mile away—yet ministries still allow them to take root. Others are more obscure, and the subtleties can go unnoticed unless experience and anticipation can envision what the possible long-term outcome might be.

Anticipating what issues might take hold to eventually become quagmires is, of course, the first step toward avoiding problems. Three questions can be helpful to leaders in determining if a situation could become a potential conflict of interest, and while positive answers to any or all of these questions don't necessarily assure the issue is a conflict of interest, they should trigger further examination of the situation:

1. Would it be awkward to explain?

A wise leader must internally be measuring every decision against the standard—"would it be awkward to explain this to a larger constituency?"

The unique compensation arrangement for an employee, planning retreat at a resort, business relationship with a brother-in-law, or membership to the country club may all be perfectly legitimate decisions. But, if it would be awkward to explain them to the rank-and-file employee, or at least the entire board, they are issues that could become a conflict of interest.

The CIA understands that the greatest risk to national security is not a purposeful traitor, but rather, a loyal agent who lives with a personal secret that could compromise their authority within the agency. In ministry leadership, our decisions are not of the type that could be held for ransom, but if we would be uncomfortable exposing any action to a broader circle, a potential conflict of interest may be lurking.

2. Would it limit options?

The leadership team of a large, complex ministry was thrilled to find an insurance broker who could address the complexities of their needs, understood the international distinctive of their staff needs around the world, and had a heart for ministry. When evaluated against several packages of insurance, this policy clearly was the best.

To celebrate, share, and pray for their work together, the president of the insurance company invited the senior leadership of the ministry to spend a few days on his luxury yacht. It was an exotic adventure unlike any vacation they had ever experienced, and all were wide eyed in response to the firm's generous hospitality. The ministry believed they were off to a great start with this new insurance supplier and ministry advocate.

The cruise turned into an annual getaway, and three years later, when the ministry would normally rebid their insurance, it just didn't seem proper to question the rates, so they waited. And a few years after that, it still didn't seem right to examine if they were getting the best deal while they were being treated so well. So nearly a decade into the relationship, when they did raise the question and the broker responded with indignation, they realized that their potential conflict of interest had become one.

Does it limit your options for future decisions if your banker is a major donor, your lawyer is in your Sunday school class, or your architect is a relative? Are your options limited because you are fearful that reexamining your retirement plan will offend your long-term agent, questioning an expense report might be uncomfortable for a senior leader, or saying no to a board member's bad idea might limit future giving? If any relationship restrains options for future decisions, the issue may inherently harbor a potential conflict of interest.

3. Would it provide an incentive?

It is amazing how much we are willing to give up for so little. Are the bonus miles earned from a big airline really worth giving up the savings of a discount airline ticket? Is a "free" fifty-dollar iPod of higher value than not comparative shopping for bulk cleaning supplies? Are four annual tickets from your financial advisor to a major league baseball game worth not questioning the indexed market value of your endowment return?

Those rather obvious examples of incentives are repeated often in ministry, along with others that are not as blatant:

- The three-day conference becomes more of a priority when you realize it is held in the town where your aging parents live.
- A consultant is retained not as much for what she knows, but because you understand her recommendation will be critical for an eventual career change.
- Overpaying your administrative assistant assures you are well protected by the front line of defense in your office.
- Developing a new training program is a tough sell among your overtaxed leadership team until they discover that teaching in the program pays them a stipend.
- Allowing one of your senior leaders to have an additional month of vacation paves the way for you to take one as well.

Any personal advantage gained by anyone, no matter how small, could be fertile ground for a potential conflict of interest.

Freeze Frame

Early on in their career most leaders learn to recognize potential conflicts of interest or at least get an uneasy feeling about a situation that could become a difficulty. But unlike traditional problem-solving patterns, recognition of the issue does not get you halfway to the answer, and awareness does not lead to the solutions to these problems. The tough challenge with potential conflicts is not in identifying the problem, but in taking action. Because these solutions require remarkable insight, wisdom, and courage, leaders tend to freeze and not act, even when able to clearly identify the root problem.

Leaders intertwine five justifications that keep them from action that will resolve a budding conflict of interest:

1. Optimistic Expectations

No matter how many times a leader has been burned from a conflict-of-interest problem, they always assume next time the results will be better. Leaders tend to be optimists by nature and thus rationalize that the earlier conflicts were only a unique situation gone awry, and the pattern won't be duplicated. So rather than address a question fully, their idealized outlook assumes the best in everyone involved and freezes their willingness to act.

2. Short-Term Benefits

Leaders allow potential conflicts of interest to go unaddressed because ignoring the issue often brings short-term benefits. Insider business deals, incentive-based decisions, or pledges with strings attached may allow a ministry to make progress in areas of need. The attraction of short-term benefits freezes leaders from actively addressing the potential conflict of interest that could become difficult.

3. Complex Relationships

Potential conflicts of interest nearly always involve complex relationships with board members, key employees, large donors, or long-term vendors. When relationships are straightforward, they rarely have the potential to become difficult. But multilayered entanglements keep leaders from digging into knotty situations, and other times the strong personality or even bullying of the other party freezes the leader from acting.

4. Borrowing Trouble

Because conflicts of interest always involve complex relationships that are difficult enough to deal with straight up, the thought of prematurely addressing a problem that may or may not become a difficulty is not appealing to leaders. Rather than opening a can of worms, leaders tend to freeze and wait until the problem develops in full. But then of course, once a potential conflict of interest has become one, it is many times more difficult to solve because it is entangled in a complex relationship.

5. Hard Work

It requires purposeful additional effort to avoid situations that could develop into a conflict of interest. Bidding a purchase, assuring equity of benefits, or addressing the pitfalls of a board-member business deal all take time, effort, and emotional energy. It is easier for leaders to work within convenient relationships and opportunities rather than root out conflicts before they develop. In most cases, a combination of these five justifications are in play as leaders face a potential conflict of interest, although any one of the five alone has the strength to freeze a leader's actions.

Taming Tigers

Understanding how widespread the dangers of potential conflicts of interest are in ministry, leaders could feel like a tiger tamer working without protection. Holding the tiger by its tail allows the tamer to keep some level of control, although both the man and the dangerous animal are fully aware who controls the situation, as the tiger could turn and bite at any time.

The obvious question must be asked: Should a leader avoid all conflict-of-interest situations? Ideally the answer is yes, but practically in ministry, it would be impossible. The sphere of a ministry is too small and interconnected for leaders to run from every potential conflict of interest. Moreover, ministries find they get better service, prices, and advantages by working with people who have cross-related connections and shared Christian commitment, and to forgo those opportunities may not be good stewardship. Rather, leaders must put safeguards in place to assure their potential conflict-of-interest relationships do not become a problem, just as a tiger trainer needs a strong stool, sturdy chair, and powerful whip if he is to work in a treacherous environment.

Strong Stool—Transparency

Thorough transparency is the framework for preventing a potential conflict of interest from becoming a problem. Whenever relationships are hidden, unspoken, or guarded they will become a problem, while difficulty is usually avoided if issues are fully disclosed, accountable, and discussed. Although a probing dialogue may be awkward at the beginning of a new connection, that discussion is much easier than the emotional confrontation required to resolve a difficult conflict later on.

To the extent a leader feels compelled to avoid talking openly about a potential conflict up front, the higher the likelihood it will eventually become a problem. This is a solid gauge to know whether or not the situation should be avoided altogether. If the relationship does not provide a framework of trust strong enough to tolerate an open discussion of potential conflicts at the beginning, then it surely cannot sustain a happy resolution should a full-blown conflict of interest develop.

It may be uncomfortable for a leader to initiate the discussion of potential conflicts of interest, but that heart-to-heart talk is vital to protect all parties from a tragic outcome in the future.

"If you construct our new building, let's make a plan now for how to separate our friendship from business in order to handle the eventual sharp disagreements that are organic in every construction project."

"Should you become our agent, how can I be assured you will be comfortable when we rebid the insurance every three years?"

"I'm happy to talk with you about your offer to get our business, but I don't want to do that if we can't still be friends should we decide to not use your company."

There is no shortcut to the difficult thirty-minute dialogue that needs to take place at the first inkling that a potential conflict of interest is on the horizon.

The best leaders will follow up that conversation with a written summary of the discussion, to ensure no misunderstanding of expectations and understanding. These issues are too important to leave to ambiguity, and the more these questions are evaluated, articulated, and agreed up front, the more likely it is that a potential conflict of interest will not become one. After a conflict of interest becomes a problem, emotions run deep, justifications become entrenched, ownership takes hold, and fences get built—while at the outset of a relationship, everyone is anxious to make the situation work despite the inherent land mines, and willing to make provisions at that stage that would never be considered later.

Sturdy Chair—Support Structures

One of my priorities in building a board is to assure that the membership includes two bankers and two lawyers. The insights brought to the table through these professional perspectives are invaluable in protecting a leader from simmering conflicts of interest.

Bankers are wonderful gifts to ministry leaders, but they are too often feared and underutilized. These folks see the world differently from the enthusiastic, trusting, and best-scenario-projecting nature of ministry leaders. Bankers are trained and paid to project what could go wrong, articulate the starkness of reality, and focus more on what has been, rather than what could be. Quality banks are built by people who have learned to minimize risks by projecting the downside to every venture.

Bankers on a ministry board bring voices of balance, caution, and an experienced nose for sniffing out conflicts of interest that could become difficulties. When a banker offers caution about relationships, the caution should be considered, and if valid, the banker's concerns can be an appropriate justification for not going forward with the relationship—rather than the leader carrying the brunt of that decision.

Two bankers on a board is important so that a single banker does not create a conflict of interest—and has a peer in the room to assure that does not happen. Also, because some bankers are more cautious than others (all of them are cautious), two levels of diligence can bring additional insights.

The same pattern is true with lawyers. With lawyers, their specialty is so unique, one who has background in corporate law and another who specializes in personnel is the ideal mix. Lawyers primarily work with situations that have gone bad, and thus their vast experience can help protect a ministry leader who wants to assume the best of everyone. Further, the response "Our lawyer believes we must not give you a special exemption to the employee benefits plan" ends the discussion and protects a ministry leader from standing alone in the decision.

Other structures are available to ministry leaders, both to provide wisdom and to carry the decisions avoiding potential conflicts of interest. Auditors can be a wealth of help as they work within the regulations they must follow. But also inviting them to aggressively guard against potential conflicts of interests can save everyone difficulty (e.g., any CEO who does not encourage the auditor to review their personal expense account is not taking advantage of a helpful structure already available).

The audit process is enhanced by the CEO meeting with the auditor without the CFO in attendance, as well as board members meeting alone with the auditor without any paid staff present. An audit committee comprised of those who have no board or staff association with the ministry will get the most from the audit process and protects the ministry on many levels, including avoiding conflicts of interest.

The executive committee of a board is another structure that can help protect against conflicts of interest. The great advantage of a smaller group compared to most formal board meetings is their willingness to transparently discuss complex, personality-based problems. Especially if the potential conflict of interest is with another board member, this group can be helpful in solving the problem.

In the Christian leadership world, two external groups also provide resources for helping to shoulder the burden of avoiding conflicts of interest. The Evangelical Council for Financial Accountability offers standards and practices that, if followed, are an outstanding resource for protecting against conflicts of interest in finance, fund-raising, and board governance. Additionally, sometimes a voice of experience that has no connection with your ministry is a vital sounding board in avoiding a potential conflict-of-interest situation. The Christian Leadership Alliance is the best crossroads for making such friendships locally and nationally as they bring together leaders who hold to biblical values of management. Their networks, as well as their materials, are a unique resource for Christian leaders.

Powerful Whip—Written Policies

Boards set policy on many levels, but Christian ministry boards have been slow to address the need for a conflict-of-interest statement because they assume this problem is based in ethics alone. More often than not, even if the policy has been created, it is shelved and ignored. Ministries must have a policy, include it in the materials for every meeting, and systematically ask about conflicts of interest.

The policy must focus more on the "spirit" of avoiding conflicts of interest, rather than articulating and legislating every possible scenario that could develop. Jesus taught us a framework for living, not rules by which to live, and a conflict-of-interest policy statement should also focus on the big-picture ideals rather than the law. At the same time, it should be specific enough to give board members adequate understanding of the types of concerns that must be addressed.

A quick search online will produce hundreds of policy-statement examples. This is the policy I developed with my board of trustees:

Sample Conflict-of-Interest Policy Statement

Board members must avoid any conflict of interest with respect to their fiduciary responsibility. There must be no self-dealing or any conduct of private business or personal services between any board member and Belhaven College except as procedurally controlled to assure openness, competitive opportunity, and equal access to "inside" information.

It is recognized that actual or potential conflicts of interest may arise because of the multiple interests and activities of the Trustees and committee members. However, Trustees have a responsibility to discharge their duties in good faith, with a high degree of diligence, care, and skill, for the sole benefit of the College.

Any Trustee having an actual or potential conflict of interest which might affect or appear to affect his or her position or action in any matter coming before the Board or any committee of the Board shall disclose the conflict, shall not vote or use his or her personal influence to effect the voting on such matter, and such member should not be counted in determining the quorum of a meeting at which action on such matter is to be taken. The minutes of the meeting shall reflect the individual's abstention from voting.

This policy is not intended to prohibit trustees and committee members from furnishing services or goods or otherwise entering into business relationships with the College. However, such an arrangement or contract must be pursuant to an arm's length agreement for fair and reasonable consideration, with the exception that the College may receive donated or discounted goods and services.

The Policy on Conflict of Interest is adopted for the guidance of the trustees and committee members and is to be enforced solely by the Board of Trustees.

Annual Disclosures

Like the importance of having an executive session of your board at every meeting—whether you need it or not—annually asking for the disclosure of conflicts of interest also raises potential problems before they can develop. If you only ask for a disclosure when there is a problem, the spotlight of interrogation is turned on with full force. On the other hand, routinely asking for disclosure saves the board and CEO from that eventual uncomfortable moment.

The simple form my board uses can be completed in only a few minutes at the end of a session during our fall meeting:

To: *Board of Trustee Members*
From: *Board Chair*
Re: *Conflict of Interest Disclosure*

Our board policy calls for us to regularly assure we disclose potential conflicts of interest between board members and the College. While our policy allows members to do business with the College and its employees and students, it is important that each member disclose those dealings. The Executive Committee asks all members to complete the following. Please complete the form during the meeting or return it to the President's office.

- Do you do business with the College? Please describe the nature of the business relationship and the name of your key contact person.
- Do you do business with individual College employees and/or students? Please describe the nature of the business relationship and the name of the people.
- If the nature of your business would be better understood through a discussion rather than completing this disclosure statement, please check this box, and we will set up that dialogue.

The Conflict of Interest statement of our Board Policy Manual is attached.

The Joy of Minimizing Conflicts of Interest

Potential conflicts of interest do not need to become so. Not long ago, I faced the prospect of selling property to my architect, who is the son-in-law of my former vice president for development, who lives down the street, who sings with me in my church choir, and who is a major donor to the college. Definitely playing with fire in the conflict-of-interest arena.

But we worked together through the process. We had frank, up-front discussions, applying the principles of Stool, Whip, and Chair, and came through it as closer friends who had benefited tremendously from the transaction. In truth, dealing with potential conflicts candidly and transparently will honor God's working in our organizations. And when done right, these situations will become some of the greatest joys of longview leadership.

8

Planning Will Drain the Life from Your Ministry

From the earliest graduate school lectures I heard in organizational leadership theory, through many years of patterning off what the "big boys do" in university governance and business leadership, I bought into the belief that it is impossible for an institution to move forward without a concise, clearly articulated ten-year plan that projects a bold future.

In practical terms, here's how that theory works: A new CEO, or one feeling the pressure of our "what-have-you-done-for-me-lately" organizational culture, will mount a platform draped with colorful banners and artful visuals to announce a major planning effort. The complex, multilayered structure, the crowd is told, will be completed in the next eighteen months—usually just in time for a decade marker of the organization's founding.

The implementation of the process itself includes an array of appropriate subcommittees so that no stakeholder group is left out, and plenty of room is allotted for compromise to ensure that everybody gets a little something. It is especially nice if the plan is written in a theme that allows each point to be summarized with a word beginning with the letter "P" for Progress, or "C" for Courage, or E for Excellence. The goals must be graphically presented in smoothly climbing growth projections, and contain initiatives that not only look symmetrical in the brochure, but make absolutely everyone in the organization feel "semisatisfied" with the outcome.

Finally, the ten-year goals are printed on oversized glossy paper with large pictures of happy, well-scrubbed faces (taking great care to include a picture of the staff member who was most vocal against the plan). The dozen objectives for the decade ahead will then project a future bold enough to inspire donors and make the board feel they are leading something really sophisticated.

For a quarter century I, too, followed this structure of planning; it is the most secure path for leaders to walk because it is rarely questioned. I've chaired the committees, I've appointed the panels, and I've written the documents. Moreover, I work in an industry where such meticulous planning is not only the norm, but is considered the gold standard of quality leadership.

I began to question this workhorse of leadership by systematically studying the longitudinal outcomes of my planning efforts and probing the issue with dozens of leaders. I became convinced that comprehensive traditional planning models are not only an ineffective use of energy, but the process itself drains the life out of our ministries by distracting us from our core focus. So in what has become my boldest change in all my years of administration, I gave up this type of planning in 2003—and I've never looked back. How ironic it is that perhaps the best way to be a good steward of the future of your organization is to quit reaching for it and instead begin to recognize the opportunities that God brings to you.

We Never Planned for This

This idea crystallized one day in a conversation with a seasoned college president who had totally revolutionized his campus over a long tenure. He'd built buildings galore, added programs and degrees, and expanded the college's reach to become a nationally influential institution. As I talked with him and his director of planning (of all people), he said to me, "You know, the most significant things that have ever happened to this place were never planned."

Why do we continue to rely on comprehensive planning models that not only don't help us much, but usually hurt us? Is it the expectations of the businesspeople in our constituencies? The drive for marketplace professionalism? The pressure to create bigger and better in order to raise funds? Or does the structure of planning simply offer shelter from the hard work of doing? No matter what the cause, excessive planning is draining the life from us.

Much Ado about Planning

I think there are at least three reasons for the paralysis that is created by overvaluing and overemphasizing the planning process.

First, the future is unpredictable.

Any meaningful planning process has to be built on a set of assumptions regarding what lies ahead. So either you inspire your stakeholders with orderly growth curves built on what is obviously an unrealistic future, projecting a robust global economy, no terrorist threats, and hurricanes that never hit land—or you raise fears instead of funds by basing your plans on less rosy assumptions that reflect the uncertainties of tomorrow. The entrepreneurial optimists on your board see a wide-open future, and the bankers look at the same data with doom and gloom. Both are right and both are wrong, but based on those assumptions, how are you to look into the future to project a ten-year plan? That is impossible.

Even the professionals can't get it right. A unit in time equal to six months into the future is now referred to as a "Friedman," because over a two-and-a-half-year period, *New York Times* columnist Thomas Friedman predicted on fourteen different occasions that "the next six months" would determine the outcome of the war in Iraq. And while you and I don't have to predict the outcome in Iraq, we do have to live with the consequences of events all around us that are unpredictable.

We must be looking to the future with clarity and purpose. We are not fortune-tellers, and God does not expect us to prepare for what we can't see—or He would have allowed us to see it. On the other hand, most ministries can see one, two, or even three years down the road with some assurance, and a solid plan building on that visible horizon will provide a road map into an uncertain future.

Second, the process consumes all the energy.

Have you ever seen an organization bring out its ten-year-old plan to report on the results? I haven't either, because the outcome always falls short of the plan, and the action usually winds up focusing in a different direction than the plan originally outlined. Implementation of the plan is invariably disappointing because most of the fresh energy went into envisioning a future rather than reaching it. And as the unifying spirit of the planning phase gives way to the competition of advocating for resources and priorities during the implementation phase, the process creates division and fatigue among a team.

Moreover, when the planning process is long and drawn out, the board or staff leaders who created the plan have often retired or started to move on to other organizations by the time it is ready for implementation. Not surprisingly, the new leaders have no desire to implement an inherited plan and so begin the cycle all over again by developing their own vision.

Third, your strengths are homogenized in the planning process.

Planning drains the life from us because when we make planning the centerpiece of our ministry, both the process and the outcomes must be comprehensive enough to satisfy every part of the constituency—and usually the least vital or most off-centered voices are the most aggressive hijackers of a planning process.

If you want to keep peace in your ministry through the planning process, everyone needs to be heard at the table. And any comprehensive planning process must guarantee that all issues are addressed in the end. So while your gifting may be to plant churches in Africa, your planning process is most likely to address the justifiable needs of the information-technology staff, the seminary training component pushed by another faction, the dream of your board chair to take your same model to Asia, and the demand of your finance people to build an endowment. And in the end, the overall plan includes a little of each and not much of anything. You've taken the focus off your strength—church planting in Africa—because the comprehensive planning process screams to your team, "If you don't get your requests in now, the door will be closed for the next ten years."

The Alternative to Traditional Planning

So while the pitfalls of this comprehensive planning approach are many, the question remains, if you don't follow the tradition of long-range planning, what is the alternative? Every ministry has to decide what components of planning fit for their own environment, but there are several factors important to me:

1. Developing Stewardship Priorities

It is vital that the key stakeholders agree and articulate the core strengths of your ministry that must remain your focus if you are to be a good steward of what God has given you. These priorities can address whatever is important to you, but they are not operational issues—they are the centerpieces of what you do best. This priority list of three to a dozen items allows you to keep in the center of your thinking those objectives that cannot be compromised. Include it as the top sheet on every board-meeting materials packet. Talk about it often with your team. Use it as your measuring rod. Stray from it cautiously.

2. Differentiating between Operational Planning and Opportunity Tracking

Because the accrediting agencies require colleges to have extensive written plans, we have developed an "operational plan" that includes the routine and time-tested functions we know must run smoothly in our organization. But we also have created an "opportunity agenda" that tracks new initiatives not projected in our operational plan, opportunities that come to us as God's wind blows. Keeping them differentiated on paper helps us think individually about these two very different modes that tend to get lumped together in traditional planning models.

For example, you need a solid operational plan for your development, accounting, and human resources departments. But your opportunity agenda may include an unexpected expansion with a partner ministry, the development of property acquired through an estate gift, or the realignment of responsibilities resulting from an unexpected resignation. Two distinct plans—one for operations and another for opportunities—provide focus to assure the stability functions do not get lost in the new ventures, or the limitations of operational needs do not keep you from capturing opportunities.

Recording the opportunities in this manner prioritizes your initiatives, gives form and focus to your ongoing implementation, and guides the development of your operational plan as these new initiatives become woven into the fabric of your ministry.

To demonstrate the power of seeing opportunities outside the traditional planning mode, after my tenth year at Belhaven I catalogued all that God had allowed us to do during the past decade. And the list of a dozen key accomplishments was a remarkable testimony to the ways in which the Lord had blessed us. In wrapping up that presentation, I wrote, "How fruitless destination planning would have been, for had I taken a plan like that to you a decade ago, I would have been put on the next rocket out of town."

3. Planning for Opportunities

However trite and cute the saying, the fact remains, "the only constant is change." Change bombards us daily, and life will continue to change in ways and at a pace we haven't even begun to imagine. As a leader you can bemoan this fact alongside your most pessimistic coworkers, or you can help your ministry celebrate change and rejoice in new vistas and opportunities, knowing that with every change God opens the door to service a little wider. Look for the blessings in change and share them with others. Make it part of your ministry's culture to thank God for the abundant possibilities inherent in each and every change.

This means setting aside resources for responding quickly to opportunities. Most ministries are on their heels when opportunity comes because they don't have some cash to respond quickly. Business mogul Warren Buffett bought a 60 percent stake in Marmon Holdings for $4.5 billion over Christmas break, after only two weeks of negotiation. And I've been in meetings with Bill Bright, the founder of Campus Crusade, and now his successor, Steve Douglass, when they heard a good idea and within minutes committed big blocks of money and staff to the effort. Ministries become strategic when they have reserves that allow them latitude when the wind of God blows.

Similarly, we must develop a team that is capable of handling opportunity. Having the dollars to move means little if you don't have the people with talent, experience, and spirit to tackle a new opportunity. That team won't be prepared for the moment unless the groundwork is laid months and years in advance. I'm convinced the Lord doesn't open new opportunities prayed for by many ministries because they have not yet made the investment in their people to prepare them to handle the challenge should the opportunity come.

4. Keep Your Planning Local

Planning is most productive at the local, rather than the comprehensive, level. Planning that prepares your ministry by organizing your strengths and people, and anticipating problems and solutions, is critical to success—but those who live closest to the challenges and the opportunities need to drive the planning process to get the most from the effort.

At my college, of course we don't wait for 2,500 students to show up every fall and then figure out what we want to do with them. We have careful, and often, detailed plans created months and years in advance. The difference is that this is localized planning, rather than comprehensive planning.

For instance, specific plans are developed for the athletic department as a whole, and building on those priorities, each coach drills down to develop a plan for his or her team. On a broader level, the athletic plans are coordinated with similar plans that have been created by the campus life department, the academic deans, and the finance department. All these plans must mesh together, but at every step, planning should stay as localized as possible. To do this I have used a "Facilitation Council," comprised of midlevel administrators from each key area, which meets every few weeks to assure that the local plans don't conflict but complement each other.

In contrast to local planning, ministries typically have comprehensive plans drawn up by their top-level leaders and then spend the rest of the year frustrated when the "local" team can't implement what went together so nicely when they drew it out on the whiteboard. Most often leaders need to be servants to support the planning process, rather than attempting to create the answers.

Be Yourself, Rather Than a Benchmark

Unfortunately, we are developing a generation of leaders who are afraid to make a decision without first benchmarking each issue from every angle. In the 1980s, Xerox developed the concept of benchmarking, measuring all aspects of their work against the best practices in their industry. Utilizing this concept, they found ways to evaluate each function in Xerox against the best ideas. And while benchmarking can be a useful tool for planning and thinking about our ministry work in fresh ways, it also has the potential to become an albatross impeding our progress.

Benchmarking becomes detrimental when leaders feel they must keep from promoting a new direction until they have "proven evidence" that this is a best practice. This measurement can become a crutch to take the risk out of decision making because a leader lacks confidence in his own judgment or is seeking to create "cover" to hide behind. Secondly, benchmarking is dangerous when a ministry becomes a collection of parts from other organizations, rather than reflecting its own uniqueness. Going to a junkyard to buy the best pieces of many expensive cars and attempting to refit them would not produce anything usable, even though it brought together the best parts of each model.

Dream More and Plan Less

To start where we are and determine what we can do to move our current situation to a new level is a limiting way to look at God's calling in our lives. Rather, if we will prayerfully, carefully, and regularly seek the Lord's will for our ministry, we can glimpse a picture of His desires, and then work backward from that outcome to determine how to get there.

Occasionally we see operational planning in the Bible: Nehemiah rebuilding the walls of Jerusalem, Jesus sending the disciples to prepare the Last Supper. But most of the big ideas God gave to His people in dreams: Jacob, Joseph, Abraham, the Magi, John on Patmos.

Christian leaders need to spend more time dreaming, praying, and listening to what God wants for us, rather than huddled around conference tables attempting to plan God's best for us.

It has been long quoted, "He who fails to plan, plans to fail," but don't be so sure that's true. Yes, operational, localized planning is vital to a well-managed ministry. But putting too much energy into planning an unknown future will drain the life from your ministry. Instead, longview leaders must look to the future as the wellspring of opportunity and be poised to take advantage of it.

9

Keep Your Eyes on the Horizon and in the Rearview Mirror

Jerky drivers make me nervous. I'm not evaluating their attitude but describing how they start fast and stop quickly, turn in abrupt ways, or can't seem to hold to their lane because their two-fisted grip on the wheel continually overcorrects for the previous jerky action. I don't expect the cars around me to be guided with the authority of Dale Earnhardt Jr. holding the line at two hundred miles per hour going into the back turn at Talladega, but those drivers who swerve all over the road make it dangerous for the rest of us.

When I got my learning permit at age fifteen, my dad taught me how to drive smoothly by focusing on two vision points. The first was to look far ahead in advance of the car, so I was driving to a point way down the road, not attempting to stay in between the lines immediately in front of me. And the second was to often glance in the rearview mirror to gauge where I had been and what may be coming up to surprise me.

We've seen how excessive planning can bring productivity to its knees, but there's nothing worse for an organization's long-term viability than a leader who runs his organization like a jerky driver.

Starts and stops, overcompensation, and unawareness of terrain all call into question a leader's perspective. A leader must learn that toggling between forward vision and a perspective on the past is the most assuring way to lead.

By regularly keeping an eye on the rearview mirror, we develop an insightful frame of reference for the future. By watching far ahead, rather than keeping our eyes fixed only on the road immediately before us, we can minimize the adjustments that toss a ministry back and forth.

Beyond the Longview

With respect to looking ahead, I would stretch the analogy beyond the longview needed for driving, to suggest that the essential gift necessary for leadership is the ability to look over the horizon. Like my teenager's computer game where obstacles come up quickly from the driver's viewpoint in a digital car, switching the A/B button to a perspective allowing the player to see over the horizon enables the racer to plan the right course to win. I believe this is a critical characteristic of the best leaders—seeing over the horizon to understand what others cannot yet see.

The Gallup organization has intensely studied the unique gifts of the most exceptionally talented people in many professions. They say that in baseball, one of the all-time greatest hitters, Ted Williams, could see the rotation of the stitches on a pitch coming toward him at ninety-five miles an hour. They find that the best neurosurgeons see in vivid color the various patterns of the web of nerves that look monochromatic to the rest of us. And they report that elite hockey players somehow see the fastest team sport in slow motion when they skate.[1]

In leadership, I am convinced that the exceptional are also uniquely gifted with the ability to look over the horizon. Such disparate leaders as Martin Luther King, Bill Gates, Billy Graham, Abraham Lincoln, and Henry Ford all shared the same gift—the ability to look far into the future, over the horizon, to lead to a place others had not yet seen.

Leadership Lifestyle

Developing a leadership pattern that looks in the rearview mirror while simultaneously seeing over the horizon goes beyond simple skills building. It requires a leadership lifestyle of looking back to remember, reflect, recover, and resolve, while watching ahead to anticipate, avoid, assure, and adjust.

Dual vision might eliminate much of the disappointment we've seen in church leadership over the past two decades. I'm deeply concerned that our theology of leadership has become so intertwined with American culture that we want our ministry to mirror the nightly business report with its focus on fast change leading to fast results so we can tout the next deal, product, or idea that is going to take us to a high-water mark in our next quarterly report for God. Our evangelical rallying cry has become the promotion of the next great, new thing we are about to do, rather than a celebration of what God has done or accountability for what we promised in the past we were going to do.

Too often, the message of the church is, "It will be the next evangelism tool, the next campaign, or the next new ministry that will finally win the world for Christ." But we don't talk much about accountability for the tool, campaign, or new ministry we launched a few years ago with the same anticipated results. That is poor leadership from a purely organizational management perspective, and it surely does not follow the leadership model of Jesus.

Jesus, Today and Yesterday and Forever

Jesus lived life looking over the horizon to what was to come, and from that vantage point He could see nets full of fish on the other side of the boat or a feast for five thousand people in a small basket of food, as well as anticipate a trusted disciple's betrayal or a mob forming in Jerusalem. Most importantly He saw well over the horizon into eternity and led accordingly.

But Jesus also was deliberate about looking back while creating a new future for the entire world. He was a student of the Scripture (Law, Prophets, and Psalms), quoting twenty-four different Old Testament books as He looked back to recount the spiritual framework of His leadership. He also kept an eye in the past, appreciating and understanding His human lineage, valuing physical places of significance in history, and holding great insight into the heritage and struggle of the Jewish people.

The purest example of leadership fully focused on the horizon while keeping an eye in the rearview mirror is found in Jesus. Or to say it with His words, at a level of significantly higher magnitude, "Don't misunderstand why I have come. I did not come to abolish the law of Moses or the writings of the prophets. No, I came to accomplish their purpose" (Matt. 5:17). It is especially interesting that He immediately looked back in that declaration, just after He shared the Beatitudes—which may have been some of the most radical new thinking the people of His day had ever considered.

If we would get back to a balanced perspective in our leadership, rather than allowing our priorities to be set by the sparkle of fund-raising drives, we would not only be biblically based, but we would also learn the lessons of faith that only perseverance in Christ can teach.

Our call to leadership is to "run the race"—which is several long journeys strung together as the seasons of life change, not the sprints that are tearing apart so many ministries. And while it sometimes takes a crash to change our driving patterns or leadership habits, examining the four gifts found in the rearview mirror and the four discoveries seen over the horizon may be a platform on which your leadership lifestyle can be retooled. Like smooth driving, this leadership pattern must be learned and applied consistently so that it is exemplified every time we get behind the wheel.

Four Gifts Found in Your Rearview Mirror

Every second, your eyes send twenty-four pictures to your brain while driving, so only a glance is necessary to determine if there is a vehicle in the rearview mirror. Experts have determined that good drivers look back once every three or five seconds for just an instant to have a comprehensive understanding of what is behind them. This means a driver is looking behind only about 5 percent of the time, but those minimal glances make a world of difference in moving ahead.

In leadership, that same pattern of systematically looking in your rearview mirror will reveal four priceless gifts for planning the trip ahead: remembering, reflecting, recovering, and resolving.

1. Gift of Remembering

The future is ominous—but then, the future is always ominous! When we look ahead at our challenges personally, organizationally, or globally, we say "yikes" because the unknown is overwhelming. But when we look behind, we see the route we've already traveled is much like the one ahead. And when we recount how we have overcome the unknown and unexpected challenges of the past, we can say "wow" because of how well we've done.

The Reformed Baptist pastor Charles H. Spurgeon more eloquently reminds us of this truth in his nineteenth-century devotional book *Morning and Evening:*

> Look back, believer: Think of your doubting God when He has been so faithful to you. Think of your foolish outcry of "Not so, my Father," when He crossed His hands in affliction to give you the larger blessing. Think of the many times when you have read His providences in the dark, misinterpreted His dispensations, and groaned out, "All these things are against me," when they are all working together for your good!

Leaders need to learn to glance in their rearview mirror, because success in traveling the road to the future is dependent on avoiding the crashes of the past, learning from the obstacles successfully eluded, and, most importantly, remembering the constancy of God's care. Keeping an eye on the past with rejoicing and thanksgiving allows us to look to the challenges ahead with confidence and purpose.

2. Gift of Recovering

Looking in the rearview mirror helps to measure our tempo, which we can't properly gauge by only looking ahead. By seeing the past, we can gain perspective on how fast or slow we are going and determine the correct pace that assures ongoing strength to lead a ministry forward.

A rule of thirds is an appropriate way to think of the pace you and your ministry team can handle. We have about one-third of our energy to push toward the task of going forward, one-third to put toward maintaining balance in life, and one-third of our energy that is in reserve for the occasional times when the other two-thirds demand too much strength. Thus, if a person is facing a time of exceptionally heavy focus at work, the extra energy needed will come from the middle third of the maintenance supply until that gets drawn down so far that the final third of energy reserve must be tapped. Or if there is a crisis in one's family, health, or spiritual life, energy gets pulled from the job until there is not any more to siphon, and the reserve must once again be accessed.

When we talk about feeling "drained," this is what is happening. One of the two segments of our life—work or maintenance—has taken too much from us, and if the depleted segment can't be replenished by the other, then the reserve gets tapped, and we get drained. But we can only go so long without refilling the reserve until our health, disposition, and circumstances begin to suffer. This is why those working with the demands of a White House job burn out so quickly, and victims of national disasters have difficulty getting back to work.

But not everyone is an equally balanced theoretical person. In our ministries, there are those capable of working full throttle with a 50 percent/20 percent/30 percent split by the way they are wired at this stage of their lives. Others may have that balance flipped in favor of needing energy for personal maintenance. Assuredly, everyone is different in how their energy is divided up, and everyone changes as they go through various stages of life, or as challenges and opportunities come. Only by looking in the rearview mirror can a ministry leader help gauge what is best for individuals, because treating them all the same is bound for failure, as is keeping an unwavering pace all year long. Good leaders learn the correct pace for those under their care.

3. Gift of Resolving

Some leaders never resolve problems of the past because their focus is fixed on their rearview mirror, unrelentingly reliving the mistakes. They revive each scary crash, dwell on missed opportunities, and beat themselves up over errors that have slowed their progress.

They will never move far from where they are until they turn their attention to the road ahead.

Other leaders don't resolve the past because they never look back to learn from their rearview mirror's perspective. They become overwhelmed with each new challenge ahead because they are unsure how to correct patterns and avoid repeating mistakes. They have not looked back to learn from the experiences that brought them this far, and they have no sense of proportion for the future. These leaders attempt to keep up their speed, but their continual missteps won't take them far.

Resolution comes by looking forward while also keeping an eye on the rearview mirror to learn from those painful experiences that are now behind us. I saw this in a dear friend who was wrongfully fired from a visible ministry leadership position. I agonized for him as he dealt with the blatant injustice of the circumstances and the cowardly actions of a board bullied by a few members spreading straight-out lies. The leader was deeply crushed, and his family was heartbroken as they endured torment that Christians should never inflict on each other—although it happens too often in CEO leadership changes.

In the midst of the worst of this nightmare, the question came up, "What have you learned from this?" My friend's immediate answer was to list the faults of the ministry who fired him. But in time he learned to look in the rearview mirror and see beyond the unethical treatment he had received. He resolved to discover what this episode could teach him about becoming a better leader and move forward as a stronger, wiser, and more God-honoring individual—and if nothing else, determine never to be like those who hurt him. In so doing, he also was able to resolve his justifiable anger and resentment toward those who wronged him. Such a level of resolution may even call for a time of pulling off to the side of the road to focus on the past, for it is very difficult sometimes to see clearly as we continue to speed ahead.

4. Gift of Reflecting

For a group who fervently preaches the need for personal reflection and introspection, Christian leaders are not always as dutiful when it comes to seeking insight from their organization's past. We're focused on the future, wanting to press ahead, and thus we don't take time to learn from the past. This lack of reflection shows itself in two insights missed when we don't look in the rearview mirror.

First, ministries are eager to look back to recount the successes, and in a sanctified way, brag on the accomplishments of the past. This is a good thing if touting triumphs gives praise and honor to God. But when looking back, we tend to count up the success scorecard rather than reflect on the damage we may have caused while in the pursuit of doing good.

We need to take time to reflect on the relationships that may have been bruised by moving too quickly, opportunities missed as we hurried toward our announced goals, or staff that have been battered in our rush to heal the world. This is not about resolving individual issues as discussed earlier, but instead reflecting on patterns that may have developed that harm our witness. One of the most productive Christian leaders I know never realized that he left behind a string of people who felt used up as he was charging into the future. If he only could have seen the pattern, he would have accomplished so much more.

Second, ministries are notorious for never bringing anything to an end. Whatever new program we propose today gets ladled on top of those we already carry, because leaders don't have the courage to reflect on their current offerings' effectiveness. We continue to pile on new initiatives because the old ones have missed the mark, but we're afraid to admit their shortcomings and cut them. Jesus taught us to eliminate that which does not produce results: "So every tree that does not produce good fruit is chopped down and thrown into the fire" (Matt. 7:19).

Most often our blind perseverance is deeply rooted in a difficult paradox—we first launched the effort by proclaiming God called us to it, so how can we now possibly declare it is a failure? God doesn't call us to fail, right? From that framework, giving up a project becomes nearly impossible to justify. Without reflection we will never give the careful and hard consideration necessary to understand God's timing for trimming ministry priorities, not just expanding them.

Learning how to eliminate ministry initiatives is as important as knowing when to begin one. I value the courage of my board of trustees to start new programs, and the even higher level of valor they have to stop them if we determine the program is no longer helping us fulfill our mission. Most boards cannot do that without finding fault with the CEO or staff. Ministry boards and leaders need to learn to reflect and cut free those programs that hold us back as we look ahead.

Four Discoveries Seen over the Horizon

I love to fly-fish for trout in Montana. When I first began, I fished with an old pro who used to amaze me with the way he would look out over the wide Missouri river and point out a number of fish—when I didn't see anything but moving water. Over time, though, I have learned to spot fish when they rise to the surface to gently capture an insect, and after years, I can now even see them moving stealthily underwater, barely opening their white mouths to feed.

In the same way, our eyes can be strengthened in leadership to see over the horizon, and when we learn to do so, we will discover anticipation, avoidance, assurance, and adjustment.

1. Discover Anticipation

Good leaders have a view over the horizon that allows them to anticipate problems and solutions. While most employees want to solve the immediate challenges before them, strong leaders are able to see the subsequent issues that will be triggered by a potential immediate solution. For instance, the suggestion is made often to change to a four-day workweek during times of increasing fuel prices. But the parade of problems that decision precipitates is not considered by most—e.g., productivity levels of a ten-hour workday, travel-schedule demands, answering phones/email on the off day, supporting IT systems, physical plant maintenance, equity/jealousy issues among employees, one-fourth week missed if someone is out one day sick, likelihood of long-term increased costs rather than genuine savings to the ministry, difficulty of returning to a five-day workweek if fuel prices go down. A leader who can see over the horizon would just buy every employee two extra gallons of gas for the Friday commute and keep the normal schedule intact.

The very best leaders, like the best chess players, can envision many moves ahead in the game. A good chess player might learn to anticipate up to three moves ahead in the game, while in contrast, one of the great players, Sammy Reshevsky, would often study the board for an hour to envision twenty or so combinations of moves ahead as a match began to take shape. And Deep Blue, the IBM computer that became the only opponent ever to defeat world champion Garry Kasparov, could calculate fifty billion moves ahead in three minutes.

As with chess champions, leaders who can see over the horizon anticipate the chain reaction of outcomes to understand how the decisions of today will be the best decisions for tomorrow as well. This skill may be one of the most critical components in separating those who will grow into direction-setting leadership roles from those who will always remain limited to operational administration alone.

2. Discover Avoidance

The fund-raising consultant I hired in my early years of learning the craft surprised me by one of his initial recommendations. I'd asked him to teach me everything he knew about fund-raising in a year, and then I would no longer need him. And he did just that with the understanding he would teach me as much about what not to do, as what to do. I vividly remember handing him a list of one hundred well-researched foundations I was going to approach for grants, and in fifteen minutes, he had cut the list down to seven viable candidates, telling me he just saved me a year's worth of work and ninety-three rejection letters.

In leadership, we rightfully focus on what to do, but we also need to discover what to avoid. We need our to-do lists, but we also need to keep a not-to-do list, so that the energy of our ministry does not get siphoned off into unproductive demands. George Allen, the Hall of Fame coach of Super Bowl VII team Washington Redskins, was known as the hardest-working coach in football. He kept on his television a hand-printed sign that read, "If it doesn't win football games, then don't do it." Those choices of what not to do are as important as the decisions we make about where to focus our efforts.

3. Discover Assurance

After two years in the wilderness, the Israelites came close to the Promised Land and sent spies in to evaluate the challenges and find a path forward to the battle. God was giving them this land, but He required they conquer it, which is much like our leadership charge too. Of the dozen advance men who came back to report, ten saw the challenges as overwhelming, while two, Joshua and Caleb, saw opportunity and reported, "We can certainly conquer it!" (Num. 13:30).

To provide leadership to those who can't see over the horizon, leaders need to assure others of what the future is likely to hold. Like the ten fearful spies, others will capably tackle their immediate challenges, but their view tends to be myopic and subsequently pessimistic without the demand to look beyond the current need. And like organizations of today, the Israelites talked about stoning these who could articulate a bright future where the others had only predicted doom and gloom.

Leaders who can see over the horizon don't need to make hollow campaign promises like politicians. Rather, genuine assurance based on insight, track record, and reasonable expectations will allow those in our care to work in confidence about the future. As a leader, you must assure others of what is over the horizon and share that vision with the vigor of Joshua and Caleb, who "tore their clothing [and] said to all the people of Israel, 'The land we traveled through and explored is a wonderful land!'" (Num. 14:6–7).

4. Discover Adjustment

I was literally over the horizon only once, and I didn't like it. Red-snapper fishing on the Gulf Coast of Alabama is world famous, and so on a very early morning, I boarded a charter boat with five other strangers to head to sea in search of this prized fish. I expected it would be a great time of sport fishing, but little did I know the captain had a private reef off the coast and, once we reached it, it was like pulling fish out of a barrel—except for the waves that made everyone sick.

As we began the long ride out to this secret fishing hole, I watched the shoreline of endless condominiums get smaller and smaller until they became only a bar graph on the horizon, and then they were gone. The view became exactly the same in every direction, as we had traveled beyond what could be seen from the land. It was very disorienting not to have any sense of where we were, which way was back to the dock, or where we were going. But the captain's global positioning system brought us directly to the desired spot, where we quickly caught our limit of fish.

On the way home, I asked the captain what he did before he had GPS to find the way. He told me about how they would use a compass, combined with radio connections with other boats that were also mapping a course in the same general direction. But he said, "If we didn't keep adjusting the course, we'd never find the fishing spot," and quickly added, "and it was hard work to be a captain in those days."

In leadership, we too need to be making adjustments in our course if we are to stay on track as the wind and waves push against us. It is important, and sometimes hard work, because over the horizon, we can lose our bearings if we are not confident of our course.

Now, Bring Me that Horizon

In the movie *Pirates of the Caribbean,* Captain Jack Sparrow declares with flair, "Now, bring me that horizon" as they set sail. Of course, we never reach the horizon because it always moves with us as we go forward.

Leaders must not wait to reach the elusive horizon before considering where to go from there. Instead they must develop a leadership lifestyle that strengthens their ability to discover what is over the horizon, beyond what others see, while also keeping a careful eye on the gifts and lessons left gleaming in the path behind.

10

Shepherding a Vision Without Scaring Away the Flock

Lewis and Clark blazed the longest, most ambitious, and well-known trail of any American explorers. Covering over eight thousand miles, their Spartan travels took them from St. Louis to Oregon and back in just over two years. Ten days into their monumental trip, the exploration party stopped to pay respects at Boone Settlement, the home of celebrated and now elderly American explorer and folk hero Daniel Boone. Nearly forty years earlier, it was Boone who took his own two-year trip to explore beyond the original thirteen colonies. Returning home, he packed up his family and convinced fifty settlers to join him to establish Boonesborough, one of the first English-speaking communities west of the Appalachians. Following what became known as the Wilderness Road, they cut some five hundred miles through the Cumberland Gap into the Kentucky Valley.

During the following quarter century, over two hundred thousand people entered Kentucky following Boone's trail, because he not only blazed the trail, but he also provided the leadership to enable others to settle the territory. Although his was a historic advance for the young American nation, Daniel Boone's leadership did not catch the public's attention until some twenty years later when his story was embellished by author John Filson.

Conversely, the return of Lewis and Clark was cheered nationally as a monumental feat. The expedition had gathered meticulous details about native people, topography, vegetation, and animal life. But after the report was delivered to the president, the explorers did not return to the west, and settlers were slow to follow. Unlike Boone, they did not establish a trail that could easily be followed or invite settlers into the new land—the leadership of Lewis and Clark may have excited a nation, but changed little in the near term.

As leaders, Lewis and Clark went so far and so fast, no one else was able to follow and use the new territory they discovered. What they explored remained wilderness for decades after they returned to a hero's welcome. Daniel Boone's adventures were also significant, but less ambitious and not immediately heralded by others. His leadership was a central factor in expanding the boundaries of the United States, because he brought others with him to secure the territory he discovered.

A Definition of Leadership

There are hundreds of definitions of leadership, and I frame mine in light of the contrast between these two historic approaches to exploring: *Leadership is pushing out the boundaries and securing the territory.* As leaders, we must take our followers with us—not just explore on our own, leaving them behind to cheer our adventures. Expanding the boundaries of a ministry's reach requires pushing into new territory, but that effort accomplishes little unless leaders enable others to secure the new land.

Good leaders must envision, probe, and then explore new opportunities. Because of their access to a broad network, anomalous perspective, and comprehensive role, leaders are more often exposed to opportunities for exploring new domains. But it is equally important they always return to inspire, lead, and equip others who can follow them and fully utilize the leader's advances. Leaders who boldly explore may be recognized for their far-reaching vision, but those who return to develop others who can go with them to implement the dream are the true longview leaders. And they are the ones most likely to make a long-term difference.

Opportunity Lost

Take the case of a leader watching advances of many other ministries into China, while he directs a small midwestern ministry that provides tried-and-true Bible study materials for small churches. In the decade ahead, the economic and cultural gravitational pull of China will control much of the world, so it is a place where the church must be expanding, and the ministry leader doesn't want to miss the wave of new ministry in this massive land of three billion people.

The leader dreams of finding opportunities to expand his rather pedestrian ministry into China—and subsequently, thinks of how much easier fund-raising might be if their ministry found a way to move beyond the well-worn path of their current calling. So through his network, he finds a way to piggyback on a trip to Asia with other leaders to see firsthand the possibilities in China. During the two-week adventure, he becomes energized by the scope of potential in China; all the while, his team at home is praying intensely for their leader's exploration.

Returning to Middle America, he receives a hero's welcome, sharing with the staff a multitude of possibilities for ministry in China. The leader tells of a thousand cities with a population of over a million people, of the openness of business to free enterprise models, and of religious tolerance that has not been possible since the Cultural Revolution. His team is fascinated by the report, anxious to learn more and to join in a shared commitment to pray for their potential work in China.

In the weeks ahead, the leader continues to regale them with stories of his exploration—but with each round-table speculation of what they might do in China, the routine process of producing the worn Bible study materials becomes more mundane. The leader's team waits for signals for how they should prepare to serve China, but their anticipation turns to disappointment as no tangible way for them to become engaged is presented. When finally pressed for next steps, the most the leader can offer is that he will be making another trip within the coming year, and until then it is not time for them to be involved.

After the leader's third and fourth Asian trips, all enthusiasm for the concept has been drained from the Midwest office, and feeling pressed, the leader is anxious to move forward or lose credibility with his team. Seeking to regain momentum, the exploring leader lays out plans to translate their Bible studies into various Chinese dialects, print materials in China, and distribute their work through a network of independent churches yet to be developed. The budget to move from exploring to implementing this new initiative is four times what they currently raise, but the leader promises new donors and partnerships for the project, which is anticipated to springboard them from a "mom-and-pop" shop into a genuinely international ministry.

These unrealistically rushed plans begin to drain energy from the ministry's core work, followed quickly by a tightening of the finances and staff work overload. Most importantly, the urgency they once shared for providing tried-and-true Bible study materials for small churches has waned. The staff, which had been lifted in their dreams for China, is now crushed under the pressure of unrealistic plans for going forward and the disappointment of going back.

Good leaders must always be searching for new ways to expand the boundaries of their ministry, or they will become stale and miss God's new opportunities. But unless they also create a Daniel Boone "Wilderness Road" for their team to follow and settle the new territory, they harm the ministry through their adventurous dreaming.

Balance Pushing with Securing

The responsibility of a leader is to maintain this balance of exploring the boundaries while providing the resources to secure the newly established territory, as well as sustain the areas currently inhabited. In the last chapter we talked about a leader's vision: He gains wisdom from looking to the past, and insight from gazing just beyond the horizon of the future. Now we get more practical. The longview leader must shepherd others toward the best future. The vision must be communicated passionately and understandably. Then the way forward must be laid realistically and personally.

No Vision Left Behind

Leaders must cast a bold vision that inspires, challenges, and equips a ministry to reach beyond its comfort zone. This demands energy, unity, and dependence on God as it pulls out the best of each individual and allows the ministry to do together what no person could accomplish alone. Big objectives are usually well articulated by leaders, being built into their DNA, and they get most energized when laying them out. But too many come up short in performance because they have focused on the ultimate outcome rather than simultaneously laying down the intermediate objectives, which connect the vision to each individual throughout the breadth of the organization.

Many leaders have become enamored with Jim Collins' idea of a BHAG—a Big Hairy Audacious Goal—and that is a good handle to remind us to aim high. So while a ministry must dream big, why is it so many fail to fulfill their BHAG? Because, in laying out their vision of the end game, leaders have not put the same level of energy into helping their team articulate and then follow the steps that lead to the BHAG or have helped each person to see how they fit in that vision. In not doing so, the big idea makes many in the ministry feel insignificant at best and unconnected to the BHAG at worst.

Big vision energizes the upper-level leadership team of a ministry, and in turn captures the imagination of their board and donors. And because those closest to the leader share a similar perspective, leaders assume all in their care are inspired by the big vision. But without a leader carefully guiding them into the wilderness, not everyone in the organization will be as enamored with the future laid out for them and won't come along.

As leaders, too often we forget we are leading a wagon-train procession into new territory, and up front, we have a very different perspective and role from those who are tending to the supply wagons at the back of the column. Our view in leadership is broad, beautiful, and free ranging, while theirs is often hampered by the dust of those ahead and focused on the back end of the wagon before them. Leaders must cast a vision that ensures all in their care have caught an understanding of where and why they are moving forward, because often their daily grind is much tougher than that of the leader.

Jesus didn't tell His disciples all of what was to happen in Jerusalem as He headed to the cross until just before they got there, or they might have deserted Him. God doesn't tell us all that is promised in our lives on earth, or we might wilt as children if we knew what was to come. In the same way, there are times leaders must put the needs of the ministry before their own stature, and not overwhelm those around them by articulating a vision that outstrips what others can handle. Among our followers are two special internal constituencies—those cautious about risk, and those whose personal responsibility appears disconnected from the big vision—both of which must be addressed legitimately.

A Dose of Reality for the Cautious

Financial-investment vehicles offered by Merrill Lynch are found in strata of risk, because everyone does not fit the same profile when it comes to risking their money. Some sleep well at night with funds exposed to extremely risky ventures, while others toss and turn even with the knowledge their savings are locked up in government-secured certificates of deposit. Leaders tend to have a high tolerance for risk, and the vision that inspires them often scares others to death. To compound this tension, leaders throw fuel on their fire by discounting the caution expressed by others, or operate as if consideration of risks was unimportant.

In dealing with those who are cautious, insightful leaders understand there will be times it is best not to share big visions because doing so would overwhelm others and limit their effectiveness. At other times, leaders must articulate the big vision for all. When they do so, they must also realistically address risk factors because the ministry will move forward only by dragging the weight of the cautious people. Being led by one who simply acknowledges the risks is a huge step for this group comprised of those who tend to believe (and often rightfully so) that leaders gloss over the risk factors and put all in jeopardy. Leaders who carefully demonstrate that risks have been considered will go far in gaining support.

For this group, leaders must contrast the envisioned changes against the cost of not moving ahead. Answer this question for your team: "What is the worst that happens if we don't advance?" If the risks of going forward are not outweighed by the cost of staying put, it will be difficult to bring others along.

A Sweeping Vision for Those Who Sweep

I've always been fascinated by mountain-climbing documentaries and the care and planning it takes to get to the summit of a major peak. Incredibly, most members of the expedition never plan to go to the summit. They have roles that are well understood, appreciated, and vital if the summit is to be reached, and many on the team are satisfied to just be part of the process without personally reaching the ultimate goal. The most successful expedition leaders have found ways to build on these important members of the team who can be fulfilled without standing at the top, and assure they are valued as much as those who do.

My board, senior leaders, and I all desire to be the most vibrant evangelical college of the southern United States, a college that also has a global influence in the arts. Our faculty, curriculum, facilities, and overall experience combine to make that possible. And while I must articulate for my team a compelling vision to prepare students who can take the serving spirit of Christ to the marketplace of ideas, if the housekeeping staff who cleans the restrooms of the residence halls don't understand how their jobs link into that vision, my dirty facilities may trump all other factors in recruiting the best students.

I regularly look for opportunities to link our vision to the understanding that each employee on our campus has a role in the big vision, and specifically spell out the nature of each person's interconnectedness. I remind my employees that on our campus each of them is a teacher (not just the faculty) because students are watching what it means to be called of God to your work—even if it is cleaning those restrooms. Further, research shows us that the condition of the

campus is one of the highest factors in choosing a college, and so our
maintenance work is truly a frontline recruitment of students. I am
convinced our maintenance team plays a crucial role in our vision to
become a college of global influence, and I look for opportunities to
remind them of their important calling.

Cohesive Boards

When pushing out the boundaries, the most disastrous results
come in the arena of the board, if handled improperly. While a
dissatisfied staff member or donor can be replaced, those among
the board who feel left behind become winded in their effort to
catch up, or hold back the advancing party. In turn, divisions can
develop that have lasting consequences. Unless the full board goes
forward together, tragedy is the most likely outcome. Among board
members, as with employees, there is a ranging appetite for risk, a
confidence in the leader's business plan, and a degree of clarity in
the calling to advance. Until cohesion is created around the vision,
pressing ahead is more likely to divide than conquer.

A ministry board must never become a legislative body—in
all my years as a college president, I can count on one hand the
divided votes in board meetings. This leadership group must be
well enough informed, equally yoked to the mission, and equal-
ized in temperament that they can act as one, not as individuals.
In fact, officially, a board member has no power at all outside
the meeting, because only as a body do members have authority.
Thus, developing the board to move together in unison, or at
least in harmony, is imperative for the good of the ministry and

for members to fulfill their responsibility to act only together and not individually.

Precise Words

Truly understanding the unique challenges and perspectives of those you lead is an important first step in advancing a vision. While many leaders are ready to move from here to action, the right words are truly critical at this juncture. The call to move into new territory is inspiring, but eventually the vision must stand on its merits, without emotion, as others do the hard work necessary to secure the new land. The excitement of ringing the Liberty Bell energized the fledgling revolution, but only the precise wording of the Constitution secured its stability. And the preciseness of those words matters because many far from the voice of the leader will respond only to what is written.

In any new endeavor, a written case statement is critical to articulating the vision—skipping this step always leads to confusion, frustration, and disappointing results. Writing this two- to five-page document provides the platform for agreeing on objectives, defining the terms, and developing a unified voice to take the vision to a broader circle.

A case statement is most importantly an internal document, even though it may become the backbone of external marketing as well. In ministry, we can get so caught up in the clever ways to identify ourselves and create marketing messages that we sometimes move far away from our initial vision and forget the potential residual harm caused in our creative marketing.

An author friend emailed me the suggested title for a new book that the marketing staff of his publisher had recommended. It was edgy, provocative, and would have moved the book to the front of any bookstore display shelf. While the sales folks loved it, I asked him if he really wanted that title read at his funeral eulogy. He changed it. One of the hard-and-fast rules I hold ensures that everything printed going off campus gets my okay before it goes to press. The message of headlines, pictures, logos, and paper quality communicates as much to our constituency as does the selection of our stories to feature. Leaders must assure that their marketing identifiers match up with their mission and message to protect the whole of what they desire to communicate.

One of the most vital sets of words you must protect is your statement of faith. Tinkering with this document should not be done lightly, as a clear and precise statement of beliefs is absolutely bedrock to a ministry. What may seem insignificant to some is critically important to others, and thus, when working in this area, it is critical to go extremely slow. Ministries who move too quickly with these changes find they advanced into new territory, but left many behind.

When possible, using statements already well established like the Lausanne Covenant or the National Association of Evangelicals statement of faith can be of great help in keeping a ministry from creating turmoil. Attacks for the articulation of theology will always drain energy from your central calling.

Selecting precise words can make the difference between exploring alone and securing the new land.

Step Up to the Soapbox

Once you truly understand your audience and have articulated your vision with laser-guided words, it's time to step up to the soapbox. Every Sunday afternoon since 1872, London's Hyde Park has been attracting speakers who stand on their soapboxes to promote an agenda. In the same way, today's ministry leaders must have a firm soapbox on which to communicate ideas that are becoming decisions.

"Becoming" is the key to this process, since communicating an idea only after it is settled will nearly always bring attacks from all sides. Rather, we must communicate at the right point in the process—on the cusp of the concept moving from idea to decision—if we expect to build an army of advocates instead of attackers. Communicating too soon creates confusion, and waiting too late develops dissension. Proper timing is critical in this delicate process.

If we are sensitive to broadening the discussion and addressing the fears that surround a critical decision, we can build a soapbox that will herald the idea all the way from the initial big-picture phase through the final implementation. But leaders must not step onto their soapbox of communication before they reinforce all four sides of the platform that holds their weight.

Side 1—Change Is Unsettling

All people struggle with change because we expect the tension accompanying change to be short lived, hoping we will soon "return to normal." In periods of change we want to brace for a brief time of renovation to clean things up and make the place more livable, but we are not expecting to be displaced into a whole new setting. When change disturbs those familiar settings, people tend to become fearful, aggressive, and judgmental. Like the children of Israel, we too often prefer the familiarity of our slavery in Egypt to the unknown of freedom and the uncertainty of journeying to the Promised Land.

Change is hard on everyone across the spectrum, from the cautious homebody to the thrill-seeking adventurer. Understandably change creates tension for the more habitual personality, but even at the other extreme, those who brag they "love change" don't cope well with the unfamiliar surroundings of stability—confirming the premise that, for all of us, change is unsettling.

Side 2—Perspective Is Personal

A faculty member in my PhD program began a semester-long course simply titled "Motivation" by declaring, "People always act in their own self-interest." He went on to tell us this was the essence of all motivation theory, and to lead anyone we must never assume otherwise. As a Christian I wanted to disagree, but doing so would only confirm his axiom, because I too was looking at the issue from my own "self-interest," believing that people must know that Christ can transform selfishness to service.

I've come to believe he is probably right, although Christians tend to move quickly from their personal concerns to that of the greater good around them once they have made an initial evaluation of a decision. Moreover, as Christ rules our lives, sanctification allows us to be filled with a heart-change that makes the interests of God our priority, rather than our self-centered viewpoints.

But understanding the pull of self-interest upon even godly people, we must address decisions from a very personal level before those in our ministry are ready to embrace the broader picture. For example, when my college began overhauling our health-insurance program, we added components that would make our people more healthy, control costs so health care could remain affordable, and provide incentives to help us all spend less. But though these were great ideas, the end users couldn't appreciate them until everyone first knew exactly how much their monthly health-insurance bill would increase.

What decisions will mean to people personally must be answered before the comprehensive implications can be examined. This is because people who are waiting for "the other shoe to fall" will not engage in discussion until the personal implications are addressed. A great idea is not enough to convince people to join you until they are shown how it impacts them specifically.

Maybe the most poignant moment in the life of Jesus was when He gathered His disciples for their last supper together. It was there He talked about His suffering to come, shared Communion for the first time ever, and reported to them that one would betray Him. In a telling response, the disciples instinctively responded by focusing on how all of this would impact them personally: "They began to argue among themselves about who would be the greatest among them" (Luke 22:24). Jesus did not scold or discount them, but directly addressed their egocentric concerns and then went on to challenge them to a calling that would lead these followers to give up their lives for their faith in Christ. Following Jesus' model, we too must deal with personal concerns before lifting vision.

Side 3—Critics Are Ubiquitous

It is impossible to avoid, outrun, or beat down the critics of the decision. They are everywhere and in everything, and secure leaders understand critics should be embraced rather than marginalized.

In nearly all levels of decisions we will have critics—not just because of the perceived inadequacies of a decision, but because some people's overarching viewpoint is naturally tedious, negative, skeptical, fearful, insightful, or questioning. And if for no other reason, we will have critics because there is a certain percentage of people who just don't like change of any type, at any time.

Some leaders try to outmaneuver the critics by bolting ahead to announce decisions before a groundswell of objections can be established. But the hurried leader will need to confront the same critics after going forward—and invariably post decision pundits come with sharper teeth.

I am adamant about sharing ideas with critics before decisions are made, because the decision can be improved by their analysis and understanding at that point in the process, rather than after the directions are set in stone. Also, it is important to address critics early on because like a spreading virus, they can quickly infect others with their skewed viewpoint. Leaders will always be ahead by bringing critics into the circle early rather than attempting to shut them out.

Our campus shifted to a totally smoke-free environment, even though we only had a small handful of smokers among our students. Before we made the decision, I sent the dean of students to talk individually with most of the smokers, and I talked to some personally, rather than let the decision announcement trigger a petition of protest. The change went through with hardly a hitch when we finally implemented the decision, because we had done the work with critics up front.

Moreover, there is usually something helpful that leaders can learn from even the most unfair, unreasonable, or unfounded criticisms. Periodically I have received one of those letters that takes "asbestos gloves" to handle because the writer is breathing fire. While the assumptions are usually rooted in baseless information, it amazes me how even in the most misguided attack, I can find some truth and learn something of value.

Side 4—Leadership Is Essential

A campus, ministry, or church cannot operate effectively as a democracy. To cater to the lowest common denominator of agreement and comfort level will stagnate any organization. But especially within the church, where boldness, purpose, and determination must drive our mission as followers of Christ, we will become withered vines without strong, godly leadership. Jesus gave us the correct leadership model as He worked with the disciples, listening, teaching, growing, and teaming with them—but never giving up His responsibility to lead them beyond what they would have done on their own had democracy ruled.

I followed closely the president of a major ministry as he unveiled an idea everyone thought was unreachable—"crazy" was the most common word I heard to describe the idea. As he shared it with his inner circle, their skepticism was enormous; as he broadened the discussion to his employees, their fears grew; and as he shared it with donors, their criticisms mounted. I assumed he would abandon the concept because, although it would represent a quantum leap forward in the ministry's effectiveness, the risk of failure was too high and the objections had become a gathering storm.

Instead of letting the mood around him rule the day, this leader didn't force his idea but patiently continued the dialogue with a loving, attentive, and listening spirit, while never wavering in his commitment to the dream. Over time his persistence began to find footholds for the idea, critics evolved into advocates, and donors responded to the challenge. His leadership never coerced agreement, but his inspiring vision, combined with a gentle spirit, had a gravitational force that gathered minds to embrace what eventually became "our" idea. Such leadership resiliency is essential for a good idea to move toward becoming a shared decision.

Communicate with Your Heart Instead of Your Head

Firmly standing on these four sides of a reinforced soapbox that respects the unsettling and personal nature of change while providing strong leadership to work alongside critics, leaders are ready to communicate ideas and decisions to their constituency. They have scouted the trail, now it's time to move out en masse. But leaders will not succeed with even the first steps unless the communication is delivered with a trustworthy and loving spirit. We must share openly, respectfully, protectively, and simply.

Communicate Openly

Sharing ideas in the developmental phase of decision formulation is one of the most important acquired skills of a leader. We naturally want to avoid opening ourselves to criticism or power struggles as well as shared credit. Those temptations must be resisted, for the tendency to hold tight always limits a leader's efficacy.

I have found that when you communicate openly in a consistent manner with those in your care, they will respond with kindness, understanding, and a desire to give the leader the benefit of the doubt. You can't have all the answers, be prepared for any question that might come, or pretend to have a problem solved. But you can promise to get the information, listen to new insights, and work together for solutions.

This open communication is not shallow poll taking that leaves people with even less voice because "now they have been heard" and have no way to take the discussion to the next level. Rather, genuine transparency demands generous give-and-take between a leader and those closest to a problem. Anything short of this is simply a way to control those who might object and will in time be seen for what it is.

If you leave meetings feeling battered and bruised, it is probably because you have yet to create the right environment for open communication. Stay the course and don't give up until you get there. In that situation it is helpful to begin with smaller groups, building trust among a few who can come together and then influence others. Start with those closest to you and work to broaden the circle. Or begin with those most likely to be aggressively critical, showing them you mean business to listen and learn. Remember, however, that while this approach can bridge the path to open communication, it can also trigger jealousies and gossip, so it is important you explain your purpose to the broader group and hopefully begin ministry-wide dialogue sooner rather than later.

Communicate Respectfully

Some people know how to examine the details of the world with a microscope, others use a telescope to see the big picture, and others employ an endoscope to gain perspective from the inside. Few individuals are skilled in more than one examination instrument, and no particular instrument is preferred over the other, for all accomplish different tasks. Leaders need to be thankful for all of these unique approaches because there is value in each outlook (although most of us assume our approach is best). In order to be most effective, we must learn to respect styles other than our own and adapt to those styles rather than expecting coworkers to adapt to ours.

Because no one individual is equally gifted in seeing all the pitfalls and potential of the new way forward, God gives each employee perspective, insights, and expertise, and leaders must create a climate to ensure each view can be used to make the overall idea stronger. Everyone within your circle will evaluate ideas and decisions at their speed and in their style. Some will "get it" within the first paragraph of explanation, and others will struggle endlessly. Men may see it differently from women, older employees may not react the same as younger people, and the tedious will dig deep while the risk takers will just fly over. Our responsibility as leaders is to respect each viewpoint and provide space for all individuals to work through the issues in their own way. We need their input to facilitate good decision making.

Because a leader's core job is, in fact, to make decisions, experience enables him or her to pass judgments and form conclusions much more rapidly than most people. To expect others to have the same decision-making skill set is unrealistic. Open communication about a decision will never progress as rapidly as we might like, and part of communicating respectfully is providing others with a schedule that will accommodate the process.

Communicate Protectively

During these forward advances, leaders must learn to communicate their commitment to protect the core ministry values during a time of change. Securing the boundaries is critical to assure ministry stakeholders that the foundational framework of their calling will not shift. Changes in personnel, structures, or systems must be linked back to the unshakable principles on which the ministry operates. If others are assured you are protecting what matters most, there will be more openness to the proposed changes looming on the horizon.

Christian colleges have had lots of pressure to take advantage of downtime on Sundays. Like my peers at other campuses, I have been given a laundry list of good reasons why sports teams should play on Sunday, why arts offerings should be considered worship presentations, and why activities to keep students busy is a better alternative than a blank schedule. But this is an area where I was unwilling to shift our position.

Throughout the decision-making process, I did my utmost to listen carefully, discuss freely, and respect deeply the opinions of others, and I often agreed with most of their arguments. But I could not solve the "slippery slope" question: If we open Sunday for some activities, where is the appropriate line to stop? I eventually made the decision not to shift the standard. While holding the line was not what others may have wanted, or what has become practice at even many Christian colleges, the decision was accepted, I believe, because they respected the stand to hold to unwavering principles that have been important throughout Belhaven College's history.

Based on principles we are entrusted to protect, a leader's communication must reflect a track record of credibility so that when a decision is made, those around us will know we have the skills, tenacity, and commitment to produce what we promise. As a leader it is my reputation that is on the line when we commit to a budget, design a new program, or add new positions. As one who leads a Christian organization, I am reflecting Christ—my reputation is His reputation, and I must never become unlinked from Him in ministry leadership. So while I seek lots of advice, others must have confidence that we will achieve a new undertaking if the decision is made to go forward.

Communicate Simply

The very best leaders have learned to communicate complex ideas, problems, and decisions in simple ways so they can be understood and owned by everyone.

Ronald Reagan was labeled the "Great Communicator" because he took complex national issues and shared them simply ... "Government does not solve problems; it subsidizes them."

Billy Graham was the world's most popular preacher because he communicated simply the fathomless theological principles of the Scripture ... "[People have] two great spiritual needs. One is for forgiveness. The other is for goodness."

Great leaders do the hard work necessary to learn to craft a phrase, share a story, or build an analogy that takes the most knotty ideas and shares them with simplicity. This is critical because to build cohesion around a decision we must provide "take-home ideas." By that I mean every employee may understand what you say, but until they can internalize the idea enough that they can take it home to share with their spouse, neighbors, or friends, they will never buy into the concept.

One of my most satisfying moments as a leader came when we brought to Belhaven a film crew to capture the essence of our college mission and experience, interviewing anyone who looked interesting—faculty, staff, students, and constituents. After the first day of shooting they came back and declared they had found a serious problem. They were convinced we had told the campus what to say if interviewed because, as they reported, "We are getting the same words and ideas from everyone."

They were shocked to hear we didn't even tell the campus that a film crew was coming, much less coach them on what to say. The message—preparing students academically and spiritually to

serve Christ Jesus in their careers, relationships, and the world of
ideas—had permeated every aspect of the campus.

Realizing the Future

When leaders introduce new ideas, they draw people into an exciting dream. Painting the picture of a new concept allows others to
imagine and live in the world of "what if" rather than "what is,"
and collectively strengthens the ministry's vision. Ideas pull out
the best in people and lift them out of the bonds that make them
feel restricted. New ideas unleash creativity, optimism, and energy
throughout the ministry.

But the exact same concept, when introduced as a decision
rather than an idea, strikes fear in the hearts of people as they
struggle to understand its import and ramifications. And from
varying viewpoints, the decision can simultaneously be seen as too
bold or too timid, too innovative or too conservative, too caring or
too thoughtless, or dozens of other extremes.

A longview leader must shepherd his vision and communicate
his vision in such a way as to secure buy-in from the top down,
bottom up, and side to side in his organization. Stewardship, follow-through, circumspection, endless listening, gracious tenacity,
and practical implementation are vital if you are to be a visionary
to the people you lead, rather than one who hands down frighten-
ing decrees.

11

Good Ideas Stand Up
in the Light of Day

★

Light is the dominant biblical image of Deity, and seeking the light, living in the light, and sharing the light is our calling as followers of Christ: "God is light, and there is no darkness in him at all" (1 John 1:5).

Jesus said to the people, "I am the light of the world. If you follow me, you won't have to walk in the darkness, because you will have the light that leads to life" (John 8:12). And as leaders, we must seek all the light God gives us if we are to capture the best for our ministry.

One of the strongest senior leaders in the Bible eloquently articulates the essentialness of God's light, even though we may come to our task with significant experience, wisdom, education, and skill.

> *Wisdom belongs to the aged, and understanding to the old. But true wisdom and power are found in God; counsel and understanding are his. What he destroys cannot be rebuilt. When he puts someone in prison, there is no escape. If he holds back the rain, the earth*

becomes a desert. If he releases the waters, they flood the earth. Yes, strength and wisdom are his.... He uncovers mysteries hidden in darkness; he brings light to the deepest gloom. (Job 12:12–22)

While we desire for the light of God to illuminate every aspect of our lives, it is often sinfulness, selfishness, silliness, or stupidity that makes leaders want to shield new ideas from the light of day. In sidestepping the light of evaluation, leaders not only become ineffective, but their secrecy collides head-on with their calling as Christians.

Like casting a vision, big, fresh ideas are exciting to leaders, but they must also have the humility to offer up their ideas for scrutiny. In doing this, longview leaders protect their own organization from oversights and creates in it a safe place for the best ideas to flourish. While it is tempting to leverage your position to hustle your flash-of-genius concept into effect quickly, that may be the surest way to dead-end yourself as a leader and sidetrack your entire ministry. Leaders will be most effective when they assure that their ideas can withstand careful examination; they must learn to welcome, rather than fear, the scrutiny of new ideas.

Good decision making becomes stilted when ministries tolerate a dysfunctional organizational climate that limits examination of new ideas. Good leaders have learned to develop both the process and the courage to assure new concepts will be fully evaluated and exposed to the light of day.

A Total Eclipse of the Sun

An unexamined idea is always a bad idea. If your understanding of idea assessment goes no deeper than this baseline concept, you'll be far ahead of most leaders. You would think that leaders would want to systematically squeeze the best out of every concept, but it is amazing how often they go rushing ahead with an idea, enshrouding and protecting it from the bright light of careful scrutiny.

The appraisal of an idea often becomes shielded from light because of three large spheres that, organizationally, can cause a total eclipse of the sun. As these circles overlap and block the light, the outlook for good decision making becomes especially dark.

1. Controlling Leader

Too often because of position, ego, selfishness, compulsion, inexperience, or commitment to the concept, leaders rush to implement a new initiative before it can be modified or criticized. In doing so, the idea does not have an opportunity to be improved through the perspectives and insights of others, or evaluated in the detail and distance that comes when the idea is separated from the possessiveness of the initiator.

Leaders who are sensitive about being appreciated for bringing "value added" results to the ministry are especially vulnerable to a pattern that keeps good ideas in the dark until they are ready to be unveiled to jaw-dropping thankfulness and thunderous applause. Their thinking goes, "Because my worth as a leader is measured by what I can bring to this ministry, then I must single-handedly find ways to develop the ideas that others are unable to see." That is not leadership, but arrogance—although I think every leader must fight this false voice because, if we are candid with ourselves, all leaders sometimes question the "value added" they bring to their ministry.

2. Gorilla Influencer

A small Christian college was thankful to have one of the top business leaders in the world on their board of trustees—a catch normally reserved for the wealthy name-brand institutions. Another school attracted to their board one of the giants of higher education leadership who was sought after by government leaders to set national education policy. To have such expertise, influence, and strength in a single board member is something most schools only dream about. But after the intrigue of celebrity wore off, the presidents and boards of these institutions knew they had made a gigantic mistake.

Yes, they had a person of enormous stature in their midst, but that was just the problem—a gorilla was in the room. When the mammoth personality spoke, not only did everyone listen, but also no one would dare disagree. The power differential between the gorilla board member and everyone else in the room was so great, his presence blocked out all the light that could have shined on ideas. Regarding that high-profile board member, one of those presidents told me that everyone on the board became cautious about what they said in the meetings, wanting to look good in front of him. And while the president appreciated that the powerful influencer was careful not to interject in the discussion before listening to others, invariably, "As soon as he gives his opinion, the discussion is over and done."

Not just superstar board members can be gorilla influencers. Anyone who is abrasively judgmental, comes on too strong, monopolizes the discussion, or has a condescending spirit can create the same stilted environment that darkens ideas from the light of critique.

3. Timid Employee

Far too many ministries have limited their effectiveness because those around the water cooler were afraid to participate in a free exchange about an initiative for fear of offending the one promoting the idea. They knew what to do to improve a concept, and talked about it among themselves, but the climate of the ministry was such that they understood open dialogue about ideas was unwelcome by their leaders. If we are to use effectively the creative insights the Lord gives to each person in our midst, we must always be committed to openness, trust, and accountability so that ideas will be fully evaluated, criticized, and hopefully improved.

The day your employees feel they can't tell the person they report to that an idea needs improvement is the day those employees are no longer good stewards of the gifts God has given them. Or, turning that around, the day leaders try to dampen a spirit of openness that encourages thoughtful, kind-spirited, and helpful criticism from the people who report to them is the day those leaders are no longer good stewards of what God has given them.

Leaders and employees must hold each other accountable to ensure a spirit of openness that puts ideas fully in the light of day.

These three types of people exemplify more than mere personality idiosyncrasies that block our light—they underscore deeply rooted organizational dysfunctions that not only tolerate these distorted relationships but allow them to thrive. A dramatic change is needed—from night to day, or as eloquently laid out in Ecclesiastes 2:13, "Wisdom is better than foolishness, just as light is better than darkness." Leaders must deliberately and sometimes painfully break these cycles of foolishness to achieve what is best for their ministry and God's purpose.

While any one of these personality types can obstruct the light of critique, ministries that tolerate one such sun-blocker tend to allow all three to roam their halls. And in fact, these individuals feed off of each other, and then they multiply. Like mice, if you see one, you probably have lots more in your walls. Creating an environment where these personalities can't prevent an idea from being fully examined is the foundation for good decision making.

Daylight Saving Time

Before automatic cameras made photography a mindless exercise, I loved the complexity of shooting good-quality photographs. I was proud of an expensive Nikon light meter that would measure the amount of light on every aspect of a subject I was shooting. While it was easy to be lazy and leave the light meter in my camera bag, assuming I could measure the light from experience, I found that when I learned to use the measurement tool regularly, the quality of my photos increased many times over.

The same is true as we shed light on our ideas. Five "light meters" have helped me make drastically better decisions when I take the time to use them.

1. Is the possessiveness gone?

An idea cannot take the first step toward seeing the light of day until it has shifted from being my idea to becoming our idea. Those who develop ideas want credit for them, and it is right that we recognize them. But when the originator will not release an idea so others can freely touch and improve it, the idea is bound for failure.

I was working with the executive vice president of a $50-million-a-year ministry, and we had extensively talked through a nagging problem that had threaded its way through the ministry for nearly a decade. The point of tension had become overwhelming, even though the original dream that spawned the problem was a product of genuine breakthrough thinking.

The EVP explained to me how the original idea was failing because the marketing people hadn't pushed it enough. He was further convinced the frontline ministry team didn't "get it" and the president didn't embrace it enough to bring resolution. He was able to detail the shortcomings of everyone who had worked with this idea. Finally, with unintended self-disclosure, he said in frustration, "This was my idea, and they've all forgotten who thought of it."

We may love our ideas, but holding on to them is the surest way to guarantee they fail. When we clutch an idea too closely, we can't examine it ourselves with clarity, others can't see and buy into it, and most importantly, it can't be remade into an even better concept as it is combined with ideas from coworkers. One of the reasons that Apple computer has outstripped its competitors with fresh and effective ideas is their team approach to product development. No one is allowed be possessive of ideas in the Apple environment—independence is not tolerated. And if we would adopt the same spirit that quickly releases new insights to the group we trust, our ideas would become sharper and our ministry more effective.

2. Has the emotion evaporated?

When a new idea pops into our thinking, we become filled with emotion as the initial concept quickly plays out an idealized future in our mind. The feelings surrounding the birth of an idea are wonderful, and it is part of the joy in creativity. But the best decisions are not made in the fog of adrenaline. The best decisions are made when we allow the emotion to evaporate, taking the time to examine an idea with clarity and perspective.

In 1987, as the winds of democracy were blowing across the former Soviet Union, Ronald Reagan made a speech at the Brandenburg Gate commemorating the 750th anniversary of Berlin. Encapsulating all that was happening inside and outside the Soviet bloc at the time, President Reagan posed a direct challenge to Russia's leader, saying, "Mr. Gorbachev, tear down this wall!"

That phrase was first crafted by a group of speechwriters and was included in the speech only after weeks of debate among

Reagan's most senior advisors, who argued aggressively on both sides of the idea. The phrase and alternatives were even tested on the ground in Germany and elsewhere with a host of different groups before a final decision was made whether or not to include it in the president's address. While such a challenge carried enormous risk coming from the president of the United States, the charge helped solidify the courage of those inside communist rule seeking democracy, and the resolve of the West to stand together to support them.

In contrast, just four months after terrorists attacked America on 9/11—and the fight to find those terrorists was not going as quickly as expected—President George Bush also made a statement he hoped would bring the world together in a common cause. Seeking to find broader support for the war in Afghanistan and a potential showdown with Saddam Hussein, in his State of the Union address the president called out Iran, Iraq, and North Korea, accusing them of being an "axis of evil," enabling terrorism and seeking weapons of mass destruction.

Unlike the Reagan process, the key Bush phrase, originally "axis of hatred," was developed by a lone speechwriter who never expected the idea to survive the drafting stage; it was examined only by the advisors closest to the daily, tension-filled fight against terrorism; and at the last minute, in the emotion of the moment, the president changed the phrase to the much more charged "axis of evil." The negative response of critics all around the world was enormous, impeding U. S. efforts to build a coalition in the following months.

Both statements were bold, risky, and blunt—and both were accurate. Reagan's speech worked because it was not delivered until the emotion had evaporated from the decision, while Bush's statement was considered only in the intensity of the fight. While leaders would never want passion to be removed totally from an idea, the emotion that blurs critical evaluation must subside before we are prepared to make the good decisions.

3. Has the implementation been detailed?

I once had what I thought was a blockbuster idea. My concept would give every student at Belhaven College a cross-cultural experience, build cohesion among each new freshman class, and add a "wow" distinctive in our educational program.

I imagined every first-year student and faculty member going to Belize for a week before school started in the fall. Belize is not too hard to get to from Mississippi, it is a very safe country, and there was strong support from ministries for doing significant work. The location would still provide enough "culture shock" to enable students to experience what it is like to live in a contrasting setting, and would pull students and faculty together in cohesive learning and ministry teams.

It was one of those ideas that hit me with enough force that I felt it was a winner from the first moment. I remember that night I stayed up late researching all types of ministries in Belize, air carriers that would reduce the travel time and costs, and State Department insights that would be important. I went into the office the next morning extremely excited about the prospect of what this idea could mean for our campus—to have a shared cross-cultural experience for ministry would be the perfect way to begin an education at Belhaven. The opportunity encompassed all we cared about in our commitment to service, community, learning, and a Christian worldview.

The first two vice presidents I saw that next morning "got it," which confirmed it was headed in the right direction. They became energized about the big picture and the outgrowth of opportunities. They started to layer on other benefits that could come with it, and we began to broaden the concept. I called a couple of donors who cared deeply about missions and evangelism, and they were ready to fund it to get us moving.

God was clearly in this, it seemed. This dream could really happen, I thought. I began to imagine not if we could do it, but how fast we could get it implemented.

Building on the momentum of the moment, I rescheduled appointments and cleared time to meet with the student-life team whom I would need to implement this amazing idea—and my dreams came quickly crashing down. Their immediate concerns were endless:

If we took every freshman on the trip before school started, how could we have new student orientation and not cut short the summer work schedule for students? Would this ruin the chances of students trying out for fall athletic teams because they would miss a key week of practice? What do we do about students who couldn't go because of family issues? What about those who don't want to go? What do we charge a student for the trip if they drop out of school before they complete the fall semester? How can we get enough faculty members to come back early to participate when most teach summer school and their break is too short already? Will we create retention problems among the students who can't go, because they feel they never connected with other students who shared the Belize experience? How will we accommodate the complex scheduling demands of third- and fourth-year students?

Not being one who rolls over easily when I see objections and roadblocks to a good idea, I asked the team to take a few days to detail out the implementation of the idea and "find ways to make it work." But the next week, when I saw their long list of the well-thought-out challenges and the complex solutions that would be layered onto the problem, it was evident the dream should not go forward.

When we throw light on the idea through the exercise of theoretical implementation, we begin to see the true outline of our idea. And if the path forward appears troublesome at this stage of development, we must be especially cautious because what we envision in our speculation is usually only a faint shadow of the real challenges to come.

4. Have the logjams been cleared?

Sometimes when trying to gain perspective on an idea, a leader may find that the best advisors are in complete conflict about the concept. A vigorous evaluation that has pushed and stretched the idea is a good thing—even if advisors continue to come down on opposite sides of the issue. But if the tug-of-war goes on too long, the emotions start to rise, the positions get staked out, and the advocacy may become too intense. At that point, if there is still no movement in the varying perspectives, you're facing a leadership logjam.

With a logjam at the conference table, a leader has several choices:

- Continue to let them tussle over the idea to see if one perspective takes dominance, although in doing so, the opportunities for bruised feelings and personal tensions are heightened.
- Probe hard questions that put one or more of the advocates into a corner to defend their position, even though in doing so, the risk of territorialism is accentuated.
- Attempt to be like King Solomon, and look for exceptional insight, calling for a sword to "cut the baby in half," and find where the real answer lies. While that was the right leadership move in the events of 1 Kings 3, it is rare that God gives us such an ingenious solution.

I have found the best alternative is often to wait for the logjam to clear under its own pressure rather than forcing a solution.

Before modern logging equipment changed the historic ways of moving timber from a mountain to a mill, logs were gathered in a river to be moved. The logs would be watched over by skilled lumberjacks, who could walk across the tops of floating logs as if they were on dry land, using their poles to guide the huge trees in the river's current.

But if the mass of logs hit a low spot in the river, or if a bend in the river was too sharp or a dead tree had fallen too far into the flow, the logs would begin to jam up together, and once they came to a halt thousands of logs backed up. Lumberjacks could risk their lives to break it up, trying to pull the key-pinched log free, or they could wait for the current to build up behind the pressure of the other logs until the jam broke free on its own. For their safety, they obviously chose the second option whenever possible.

When advisors get logjammed, leaders must sometimes rush in forcefully to break up the tension before a professional conflict turns personal. But in most instances, ideas remain the focus of the spirited dialogue. Even then, Christian leaders assume their commit-ment to godly peacemaking calls for them to rush in with solutions, rather than waiting for the tension to clear under its own pressure. In doing so, not only is the group not trusted to work together to find God's direction, but the leader gets hurt in the process by having to take sides before the issue has been fully aired.

I've found that taking a simple break is a wonderful tool for clearing these logjams. Sometimes a short amount of time will do it, and other times it takes weeks. But more often than not, if I wait for the logjams to clear of their own pressure, they usually do, and the insights about the idea become crystallized. When the players in your discussion have time to step back from the intensity of the moment, they tend to see each other's viewpoints more clearly, loosen their grip on their own positions, and begin to gravitate around a fresh perspective rather relying on their first impressions.

There are times I've stopped meetings in midsentence when I thought it was getting too intense, and stood up to call for a Diet Coke break. When we came back around the table twenty minutes later, we quickly found agreement. Other times, waiting for the logjam to clear about an idea has taken days or even months.

We find this in boards, too. In nearly two decades of the college presidency, I can remember only a handful of times we did not have a unanimous vote on an issue. If there is a logjam in the board that would divide the members, more time is needed to clear it and deeper examination of the idea is critical.

If a leader faces a logjam with trusted peers, and after time it doesn't clear on its own, avoid using dynamite—the lumberjack's last resort. A stubborn logjam probably indicates there is something askew at the core of the idea, and the concept needs more intense evaluation before going forward.

5. Is your intuition confirmed?

My board chair once gave me the most helpful insight I've ever had in the area of college finance. We were facing a pressure point because a financial report missed a major piece of information and the error had put us into a scramble. Charles Cannada had been the chief financial officer at WorldCom back when things were done right, before the company came crashing down. He had worked with huge, complex financial reports in the billions of dollars, and so I asked him, "How do you know when a financial report is right?" I figured he had all kinds of complex benchmarks, formulas, and checks and balances to assure a financial report was right in every detail. His answer shocked me—"When it feels right."

Big, complex issues often come down to intuition, and good leaders learn to know (and learn from others) when it "feels right." And when it is not yet right, God checks us to look further until our intuition is confirmed. If a financial report doesn't feel right, then it needs more probing until you either know it is right or find the error. If a tough personnel decision doesn't feel right, then push deeper and wait to act until you get the assurance your solution is best for all involved. When a new initiative feels rushed instead of right, it probably is hurried.

As leaders, we must commit to always being stewards who are willing to shine all the light we can gather on our ideas. And if they stand up to the light of day, they will feel right and give us that deep, settled peace that only comes when we have assurance we are being true to God's guiding.

Half the Race Is Run After the Light Turns Green

If an idea is worthy, it will withstand scrutiny, but if it can't stand up to the light of evaluation, there is no way it can stand the test of time. That being said, how often do we get an idea and run to implement it before others can poke holes in our concept? Most ministries by nature spend a lot more time cleaning up bad ideas than they do implementing good ones. Our challenges from the outside are too great to be creating problems of our own on the inside. Slowing our excitement and examining our ideas with the five light meters of evaluation can save us much.

But when we do get the green light to go forward with a solid decision, only half our work is done and the hardest part is yet to come. Now we must communicate the idea to the internal and external constituency so they embrace it with the same enthusiasm we feel, applying the principles from the previous chapter.

12

Creating a Longview Culture

The magician's audience applauds halfheartedly when he pulls a white rabbit out of a black top hat. They all know a rabbit was tucked away in the hat, and black powder that covered the animal to hide it from view was gently shaken off when the magician lifted the rabbit from its hiding place. But when the magician returns to the hat to pull out a second rabbit, the audience starts to take notice. When the third and fourth rabbits come out of the same hat, people are amazed at the skill of the magician and are talking among themselves, asking how these things could be done. If a half-dozen rabbits appear, they believe the magician can do the impossible, and buy season tickets to the performances.

After seeing the trick in subsequent performances, the same audience still appreciates the magician's skill, but the trick is becoming mundane to them. More rabbits, or a bigger animal, or something that clearly would not fit in a hat is now what it will take to gain their applause. The same feat that amazed the audience at first has become routine, and only a new twist on the old pattern could intrigue them now. The admirers begin making comparisons between what they are watching and other magicians they have seen or heard about who could do this hat-and-rabbit trick in more remarkable ways. The magician onstage is even measured against fictionalized benchmarks, as the audience remembers from Saturday morning cartoons Rocky and Bullwinkle, who were able to pull most anything out of the hat—and if they couldn't, were yanked from the stage with a gigantic hook.

Even though the magician works faster to try to regain the applause of the audience by speeding the pace of producing more and more rabbits from the hat, the audience has become disappointed and disgruntled. The magician who once awed his audience now frustrates them, as he appears to have run out of rabbits before the show is over.

The Hat-Trick Dilemma

Leaders love to dazzle their constituency with surprises that bring value-added change—and the more audacious the better. Certainly those who have gifts to see and capture these types of dramatic advances are rewarded as strategic change agents for their ministry. But when leaders build their worth from their ability to "pull rabbits out of hats," they quickly run into difficulty for five reasons:

1. A leader's supply of surprising innovations will always be depleted before the responsibilities are fulfilled.
2. Organizations cannot absorb continuous change, so the frequency of opportunities for a leader to bring value-added tricks tends to diminish over time.

3. If each "rabbit" is not bigger than the last rabbit, the audience becomes increasingly jaded and skeptical of a magic-show pattern of leadership.

4. In organizations it is impossible to be successful with every attempt, and thus any failure is magnified if leaders have trained their audience to watch for rabbits.

5. A constituency appreciates the advances created by a leader but eventually becomes resentful that this pattern frames the spotlight on the magician.

Leaders must make a game-changing difference for their ministry, but when a pattern of producing surprises becomes an expectation, the outcome will nearly always be disastrous. On the other hand, too often leaders find a ministry is in such desperate need of help that only remarkable action from a leader will pull them back from the brink of tragedy.

The dilemma: If the leader doesn't move fast to single-handedly solve problems, the ministry will suffer—but when the leader brings significant fixes, the expectation is built that the surprise solutions will continue and will swell in their magnitude.

No matter how perplexing the dilemma, a leader who chooses to follow the pattern of magicians will nearly always be limited to short-term success. Both the leader and the ministry are at fault for creating this dysfunctional pattern of leadership, although the leader can more easily rectify the situation. Ideally, the problem is avoided because boards, staff, and constituencies have a balanced perspective of what they need from a leader and straightforwardly discuss those expectations so that leaders do not feel the pressure to slip into this faulty pattern. But too many ministries are facing such desperate challenges that they hire and reward magician-style leadership for chasing after quick-fix solutions rather than long-term stability.

On the other hand, leaders must be able to pull a few rabbits of out their hat—especially in times of challenge. Those fast successes are occasionally essential for a ministry to survive, and serve as accelerators in reaching the full agenda. Thus, when needed, even "hat-trick" leadership can be broadened to get the most from the leader's results, while preventing serious pitfalls:

- Leaders must not do the tricks alone but include others so the group has ownership in the process and the spotlight is shared.
- With each new trick, a good leader keeps it in balance so that unrealistic expectations do not take root.
- Leaders who specialize in these tricks as part of their leadership package need to do them when least expected and purposefully avoid any systematic pattern.
- At the times when these surprises do come from a leader, the event itself should be downplayed and framed in context of the overall work of the ministry, not as a standalone success.
- Leader-dependent solutions should be viewed as moments to mentor, teach, enable, and equip others for success so they too will learn how to manage unique opportunities.

Leaders tend to resist this broadening of their base when bringing about unique advances—and instead stay in the spotlight because of the nagging fear they will not be appreciated, respected, valued, and compensated appropriately. But as we have seen, giving away the credit *never* hurts a leader in the long run, while hoarding the credit always does.

The brand-new president of a well-established and effectively run ministry was at risk of losing his position when I was asked to counsel with him just weeks into his tenure. For several hours we broke out a number of issues that had created his rocky start. Then finally, in a moment of frustration and candor, he said, "I've been here three months, and I haven't been able to make one big thing happen to let them know I'm worth it." He went on to describe a pattern of magician-style leadership that had always served him well in the past—although his resume showed a long line of short-term positions. But this time the ministry didn't need to be urgently "fixed," so this leader's pattern wouldn't work because he was convinced his value to the ministry was dependent on the number of rabbits pulled from his hat.

Leaders must lead themselves first—putting in check the draw into this fruitless pattern of short-gain leadership. But resisting the temptation to be a magician is only a Band-Aid fix because the lasting solution is found by creating the right organizational culture that transcends a monolithic focus on the leader's successes, creates a balanced view of long-term growth and stability, and builds systemic success into the breadth of the ministry team. Creating a healthy organizational culture is critical to allow this level of mature leadership to thrive.

Shaping Organizational Ministry Culture

The joy of international travel is not seeing the sights but experiencing a diversity of cultures. Understanding the dynamics of regional uniqueness is the starting place for grasping insights into organizational culture.

The people of Thailand and Sweden do many of the same things in daily life, but they do them in very different ways.

The music, food, and language of Argentina and Japan are starkly different, but each country is comfortable with what they know and love.

The culture differences of Saudi Arabia and the United States must be respected doing business far from home, even if one disagrees with the other culture.

Cultures that are isolated, such as China and Russia, change much more slowly than cultures with outside influences, such as South Korea or Hungary.

Just like countries around the world, every organization and every ministry has a distinctive culture. The best organizations and companies create a purposeful culture that permeates every level of operation, messages, priorities, and personality. The most distinctive corporate cultures can be summarized in a single word: Starbucks is mellow; Disney is happy; McDonald's is consistent; Wal-Mart is inexpensive; Google is experimental; Volvo is safe; Apple is innovative; Southwest is fun.

Organizational culture is the fusing and interplay of values, traditions, style, priorities, energy, worldview, attitudes, and assumptions. It is more often inherently understood and informally passed on rather than articulated and promoted. It is as much about emotion and attitude as it is about facts and decisions. It is visible and invisible; it networks together a wide scope of organizational issues large and small—work ethic, dress code, mission, values, printed logos, hallway habits, hiring standards, unspoken rules, board practices, job titles, and budget priorities. It is developed over lengthy periods of time, permeates the organization in every aspect, and is a strong tide against which few can swim.

Purposeful organizational culture in a ministry sharpens vision, creates cohesion, and frames standards of operation and success. It generates the conditions for a ministry to grow rather than struggle, just as the physical environment enriches or limits the development of life. And while excellence and quality are not guaranteed when organizational culture is persistently developed, mediocrity and bureaucracy are assured when it is ignored.

The Culture Builders Web site summarizes succinctly the outcome of a purposeful organizational culture:

What does an Optimized Corporate Culture Look & Feel Like?
People like to come to work
Turnover is low
The organizational mood is optimistic and joyful
The company vision and purpose are clear and inspiring
Employees are aligned with the company vision and purpose
There are no limits to the company's growth and profits[1]

It seems that leaders have always attempted to advance their ministry by pulling rabbits out of a hat, but they consistently run out of rabbits before their hat wears out. On the contrary, wise leaders take the longer-term view to success and develop a purposeful organizational culture that aligns the priorities of their ministry. This is not an easy task because a dysfunctional organizational culture is more powerful than a leader standing alone, and the culture of a ministry usually changes the leader, rather than the leader shifting the culture. When new politicians go to Washington determined to not be partisan, the culture around them reorders their DNA, and they learn quickly to accentuate party lines rather than cross them. To break this cycle, the most critical investment a leader can make in a ministry is to build a healthy organizational culture.

Ten Steps Toward Cultural Change

To shift the organizational culture of a ministry, leaders need to work purposefully and cautiously. Missteps can be costly to the leader, but success in guiding a ministry through this maze toward a stronger culture is well worth the risk.

Some have advocated that organizational culture cannot change—I strongly disagree. I've been at the heart of dramatic cultural change in my own institution, and I've observed firsthand such shifts in a variety of ministries large and small. It can be done, but it is accomplished only with skill, wisdom, courage, determination, humility, and prayer.

Step #1—Work within your inherited culture for a while.

The fastest flops I've witnessed in ministry leadership have had one characteristic in common—they have not respected and been willing to work within the culture they inherited. They started on day one to change the organizational culture and in doing so sent a message loud and clear that they were belittling the current culture of the ministry.

A key principle of the nature of culture—organizational or societal—is people don't want to change their current state no matter how odd it might seem to others (e.g., the Masai tribe does not want to eliminate cow blood from their diet). Thus, a leader who promotes organizational culture change at the outset is in fact attacking the values and style that are comfortable and protected within the ministry.

Unlike the colonialism of the nineteenth century, today's missionaries have learned to work within indigenous cultural distinctives rather than alter them. Ministry leaders need to do the same in order to build up rather than shatter the people they lead. In fact, a leader will not be heard in a new setting until first sending clear signals that the current culture is appreciated and respected.

When I went to central Kansas as a college president, I heard through the search process how my predecessor never put a Kansas license plate on his car because he leased a car from a dealer in another state. While the fact may be true, it sent a message to the community that he didn't embrace their culture. Thus when elected, and long before moving, I ordered a Kansas license plate for my car with the initials of the institution as my tag number, and it became the buzz of the town on day one.

No matter how much it needs to be changed, every ministry has many marvelous aspects. Until a leader recognizes those strengths and publicly holds them up before the constituency, the doors that lead to an eventual organizational culture shift will remain locked. If we could wipe the slate clean, building organizational culture would be much easier. But except for a start-up ministry that begins with a dream and a blank piece of paper, all other leaders inherit a culture that cannot be disregarded, disparaged, or dismissed.

Step #2—Look to the longview.

Changing a ministry's organizational culture takes time—not months, but years. Thus, leaders don't need to hurry the process. Going quickly won't get you there faster, and in fact, rushing may lengthen the process because the ministry feels threatened. So take time, work deliberately, and enjoy the quiet and subtle changes in organizational culture that will begin to take root.

A friend from Slovakia, and former Bible smuggler before the end of the cold war, was traveling by train during the year after communism fell in his country. He was sharing a compartment with two other travelers, and all three of them began to hear a light fixture overhead buzz, and then watched it flicker. They all watched the lightbulb for a number of miles, until my friend finally stood up and quickly tightened the bulb to repair the problem. One of the other Slovakians traveling with him, who had never known any culture other than communism, said, "I would never have thought to do that myself, rather than report it to the authorities."

Culture changes in society and in ministries mirror the same pattern. The culture of the former Soviet republics has changed dramatically in recent decades—although change in those first years was inch by inch. Those who take a longview to cultural change find these shifts begin to take on a momentum of their own, and the quickening pace of change once the new ideal is embraced soon compensates for the slow steps at the beginning.

Step #3—Demonstrate agreement of values.

I sometimes wonder how the church stays together when the styles, vocabularies, and outlooks of various denominations are so drastically different. But of course, it is our agreed commitment of faith in Christ that allows us to transcend those differences. If we are assured of what we share in common, then we are more willing to respect our differences.

Even if the style, vocabulary, and outlook of a new leader appear foreign to a ministry, both the ministry and the leader can avoid a culture clash by taking time to embrace the agreed values that connect them. When I first came to Belhaven College as president, we were primed for a dramatic organizational cultural shift—fortunately advocated by key stakeholders, including my predecessor. While our agenda for change was enormous, we were not ready to address organizational culture shifts until we confirmed the foundational commitments that tied us all together. In those first months, we spent many hours articulating our shared values, and those agreements became the foundation on which all other change could be constructed.

> WE BELIEVE Jesus Christ will be our Lord and Leader in all we say and do and that spiritual vitality, including prayer and worship, will permeate all aspects and functions of the College.
>
> WE BELIEVE quality people will be our most important resource, and that careful listening and dialogue among all campus stakeholders will strengthen our decisions and effectiveness.
>
> WE BELIEVE that quality teaching will base the principles and foundations of every academic major and individual course on biblical revelation.
>
> WE BELIEVE that the College should serve the Church through offering learning opportunities beyond degree and for-credit programming.
>
> WE BELIEVE effective and efficient administrative structures will best serve our students and employees, and are most useful when subject to critical self-evaluation and lead to continual enhancement.
>
> WE BELIEVE fiscal responsibility and godly stewardship of resources will direct our priorities, including functional, attractive, and efficient facilities that provide proper venues for quality education.
>
> WE BELIEVE higher education is a privilege rather than an entitlement; therefore we will structure fees and

scholarships in ways that will assist students while teaching personal financial responsibility.

WE BELIEVE the activities and needs of the College must be
presented to alumni, donors, friends, churches, foundations,
corporations, and prospective students enthusiastically,
accurately, systematically, and with integrity.

Those eight statements gave us the mission cohesion from
which we could eventually address organizational culture changes
at practical levels.

Step #4—Honor traditions and symbols.

Traditions matter, as do the symbols of those traditions. And
no matter how strong a leader might be, if the unique treasures
already embedded in a ministry are ignored, the leader will not be
successful.

One of the greatest rivalries in college sports is the annual
season-concluding football game between Michigan and Ohio
State, which goes back to the first meeting of these bordering states
in 1897. Fans of both schools know that nothing matters more
than beating their neighbor, with the intensity growing to such a
level that at the last practice before the big game, over 20,000 fans
attend each team's workout.

In the 1987, Ohio State hired a coach from Arizona who was vocal
about his vision to turn the football team into a national powerhouse,
rather than focusing on one late-November game against Michigan.
He did just that, taking the Buckeyes to consecutive years ranked

number two in the nation, before losing the final game to Michigan, and with it a chance to play for the national championship.

Coach John Cooper was finalist for the Coach of the Year Award for three years, finished first or second in the Big Ten most years, and sent more than a dozen first-round draft picks to the NFL. Not since the legendary coach Woody Hayes had Ohio State been so successful. But during his tenure, Coach Cooper won only two of the thirteen season-culminating games with Michigan, which was more important to most fans than the rest of the season combined. As every leader finds, traditions matter more than the overall success, and Ohio State fans celebrated when John Cooper was fired.

In any organization, and more so in ministries, traditions and symbols matter because they represent what we value. In the church, those issues take on an added dimension, becoming intertwined with how we express and emphasize different aspects of our faith. But from core theological symbols all the way to the celebration of office birthday parties, a good leader needs to quickly understand the valued traditions and search for ways to lift them up.

Step #5—Model what you expect and don't tolerate what you won't.

This is the pivotal step of the process to change a ministry's organizational culture. Leaders will get back the behavior they model.

If excellence is the standard for how to do business, make sure you hit it 100 percent of the time, and teach the value of quality as you mentor others. If a new work ethic needs to permeate the ministry, then turn on your personal afterburners and show the new pattern rather than demanding it. If you want to change the dress code, then never waver in your personal dress standard even when you just run to the office for a few minutes. If you expect high-touch involvement with those who connect with your ministry, then find ways to allow others to peek in on how you do it personally—without flaunting your behavior in a condescending way.

Change begins with this type of modeling, but it becomes ingrained through what the leader will tolerate.

If financials are to be drilled down to a level of information that will predict trends, then don't accept raw data reports. If interruptions from visitors are to be a priority, then don't continue your meeting with a staff member when *they* have someone waiting for them. For legitimate reasons, if written reports are to be completed on time, then don't be satisfied with a few hours late. If entrepreneurial ministry is advocated, then don't be satisfied with the person who gets it right every time, because the adventurous must periodically have failures.

This crucible of modeling with tolerance for what you will accept is the primary lever that will shift a ministry's organizational culture. It takes time, persistence, and an unwavering commitment to what you know is vital. In the business world, it is called winning—as expressed in *Harvard Business Review*—but the principles are the same in ministry.

Culture is not created by declaration; it derives from expectations focused on winning. You can only have a culture that encourages performance if you hire the right people, require them to behave in a way that is consistent with the values the company espouses, and implement processes that will allow the company to win in the marketplace.[2]

I attended the early-morning Bible study of a well-known author and speaker, at an hour far before my caffeine kicks in, but I agreed because of the admiration I had for the host. Despite his touring, writing, and speaking, he made this men's Bible study a priority each week in his schedule, and I arrived to a packed room of men who all carried well-worn Bibles, happy smiles, and an eagerness to get into the Scripture.

I joined a table of men near the back of the room, and since I didn't know anyone, I was a bit of an outsider to the conversation. After we went through the normal greetings, they returned to their more comfortable conversation, which quickly drifted into crude jokes and topics, cutting remarks toward each other, and a judgmental spirit about the world. I was relieved when the gifted speaker began the session and the program cut off this uncomfortable dialogue around the table.

But the disconnect between the behavior of the regular attendees and the deep public spiritual tone of the speaker haunted me for some time to come. It didn't make sense. That was, it didn't until a few years later when over a private meal with that same Bible-study leader, he also talked in ways that reflected the same language, topics, and spirit I'd heard from his disciples around the table that morning so long before.

Modeling excellence publicly while accepting something else privately will produce an outcome that follows the lowest standard of the two.

Step #6—Celebrate success.

This idea seems simple, but it truly is an art in leadership. If you celebrate too often, then success becomes trivialized. But if celebration only accompanies major events, the steps that would lead you to progress go unappreciated. Good leaders are always keeping an eye out for reasons to celebrate strengths, successes, and heritage. Struggling ministries can celebrate smaller advances—one ministry celebrated the first time they had their building landscaped in years. Others that are larger and more sophisticated can celebrate on a grander scale but have also learned to celebrate within small groups as well so that the unseen accomplishments of many are valued.

Through informal events, publications, or even my personal blog, I'm always looking for ways to celebrate accomplishments. We often honor those who go above and beyond the call of duty in their work and have achieved some unusual success. Other times the celebration is about a milestone we achieved together. In these celebrations I'm especially looking for opportunities to legitimately recognize those who do not often receive recognition. As leaders, we get appreciated often, but for someone who has never been applauded by a group, it can mean much.

A celebration that I've found especially meaningful is awarding recognition clocks at our annual dinner to full-time employees on the anniversary of their milestone of service every five years. The engraved Bulova desk clocks get bigger for each grouping of employees as we work up from five to ten to fifteen to twenty years of service. And once an employee hits the quarter-century mark we present a very distinctive mantel-style clock, leading up to the large grandfather clocks we have presented to the remarkable few who have served the institution forty years.

Celebrations must be created so that they have staying power—both in your ability as a ministry to build traditions in your celebrations—and must also be meaningful rather than programmatic. At Belhaven College, we treasure our faculty—they are a remarkable group of people. And thus we wanted to celebrate faculty who had invested a lifetime at the institution. To honor them, we created a "Legacy of Learning," which includes all our faculty who have taught twenty years or longer since our founding in 1883. At the time of this writing, forty-four faculty members have achieved that mark, ten of which are currently teaching with us today. We built a brick sidewalk through the center of campus and inlayed large bronze plaques for each honored member—with their name, academic discipline, year they began teaching at Belhaven, and their life Scripture verse. They are also given a special medallion to wear during academic regalia events.

This Legacy of Learning is an example of a meaningful celebration, recognizing the service of these specific faculty members. But more importantly, it celebrates a core value of the college—the relationship of faculty with students. Success comes from people, so our celebrations should focus on the shared mission, embodied in personalities, rather than the statistics and attributes of the achieved goal.

Step #7—Explain anticipated cultural changes.

Leaders are quick to talk about operational, personnel, or budget changes, but we tend to not take the time to explain organizational cultural changes. Maybe this is so because these issues are more complex, but my guess is our explanations have come across more like dictates demanding change than shaping guidance. Assuredly, these organizational cultural changes are multifaceted and will always generate criticism. And because of their complexity, they are difficult to summarize in a cohesive message that is relative to the full diversity of stakeholders—from board, to high-end professional staff, to operational workers. Thus, most often, leaders find it safer to be silent about cultural shifts rather than attempt to address them and miss the mark.

It has worked well within my leadership style to use a formal platform to address these type issues. As my institution has become more complex with campuses in Jackson, Memphis, Orlando, and Houston, the distances put us in jeopardy of strained relationships. And thus, we needed to purposefully deal with adjusting our ministry culture to be sensitive to the difficulty of not working face-to-face, while also purposefully assuring we create a culture of "one campus"—although in many different physical locations. I attempted to explain the organizational culture change we needed at our annual dinner that includes all of our full-time employees, board members, and key donors, as well as spouses. (Spouses are almost as important in developing mission commitment and shifting organizational culture as are the employees themselves.) Part of my speech that night addressed this issue head-on:

> I worry that strained relationships will hold us back. I think my concerns are justified because of how we have

changed so significantly as an institution during the past several years:

We've grown so much *larger*, and it is no longer possible know every employee.

We've become stretched with everyone doing more than a full-time job as we handle the growth.

We're now so *spread out*, there are people here tonight some of you work with whom you've never even met in person before because they work on a different campus.

We've become more *complex* as the operational processes must have more moving parts.

We're *faster paced* because we are rowing against stronger currents fighting Christian higher education.

When I evaluate the past year or so, I see our relationships trending toward more strained, and that concerns me deeply. Because if a steady rain of tension creates trenches of mistrust that ever get too deep and create division, then barriers of protection don't follow far behind.

The excuses of personality quirks or pressure demands don't hold up for justifying strained relationships. And with the pressure of our ten-year accreditation review behind us, this is a very good time for us to take a refresher course in how the Bible instructs us to get along with each other. You know, there may be some places where the Bible is not clear in its direction about what is the right thing to do, but relationships is not one of those places. The Scripture says:

Love is patient and kind. Love is not jealous or boastful or proud or rude. It does not demand its own way. It is not irritable, and it keeps no record of being wronged. It does not rejoice about injustice but rejoices whenever the truth wins out. Love never gives up, never loses faith, is always hopeful, and endures through every circumstance. (1 Cor. 13:4–7)

When I look at all the issues that came to me during this past year, there are so many wonderful and creative things I get to work with, but on the tough side, they only come down to two issues—money or relationship tensions. We have got to do better, not because I ask you to do it, but because it is biblical.

Addressing the challenge, and then responding with an overarching call to an organizational cultural shift, I then shared a specific implementation plan, which was built around what we will not tolerate. To complete the picture of this example, I included five specific actions: fixing relationships that are already broken; listening until you really understand; shooting straight with each other—carefully; avoiding the systematizing of relationships; committing to never start a weekend mad at anyone on the campus.

Step #8—Infuse a small team.

As a leader, you cannot shift organizational culture alone. It is critical to build a team who can carry the standard with the same authority and precision. They must be people who are highly effective and influential, secure in themselves, immersed in the vision, and unwavering in their commitment to sustain the culture shift long term.

In every ministry, there is a small group of "game changing" team members. While all employees are important, you will most likely make or break your future on a small group of key people—all of whom don't necessarily report to the CEO. To shift a ministry's organizational culture, this group needs to be empowered to work together to make that change. As they create a swirling force, they will draft others into the momentum, until, like a tornado, every employee will either be swept up in the change or hiding in a bunker for cover.

As openings come to hire new people, leaders need to look for candidates who come out of a culture that resembles what you're trying to create. If new people already have experience working in the desired culture, they can more quickly influence others and hit the ground running with a new outlook in their leadership.

With this group, the challenge for the CEO will be fourfold:

1. Delegate to them with full responsibility *and* the authority to carry their load.
2. Keep strong the relationships among them, continually mentoring and coaching.
3. Support their efforts, even when they might not do it exactly as you would do it.
4. Keep them challenged, because creative and aggressive people must be stretched.

Any leader who single-handedly attempts to bring about organizational culture change to a ministry will not get far. At the same time, waiting for the full breadth of the ministry to adapt to the change is nearly impossible. Rather, this small group of influential players is critical to the process.

Step #9—Visit models of your cultural objective.

Toyota has developed one of the most complex organizational cultures in business. They deliberately create contradictory viewpoints within the company and then challenge the employees to find solutions by "transcending differences rather than resorting to compromises."[3] That is a culture that few could emulate, and those who wish to do so should book a flight to Nagoya, Japan, because this is a culture that must be understood up close and not studied in theory.

Organizational cultural change is primarily about execution rather than being rooted in the theoretical. Thus, for a ministry seeking to make a shift, they must see how it is done firsthand, or the practical issues will draw them back to their rutted patterns of the past. When we started our organizational culture shift at Belhaven, I went to Azusa Pacific University in California to spend extended time with the president, Richard Felix, and his key team members to see their organizational culture up close. I wanted to study all aspects of what they do, why they do it, and how they execute. Then many of my team went to spend time with their counterparts as well at the California campus. Because we had much in common, and they were headed where we hoped to be, it was the right match to study. We were both on urban campuses with too little space, served an ethnically diverse student body, were not owned by a denomination but were deeply evangelical, were committed to innovation in program development, and valued a missions and international outlook.

I wanted to understand the big picture of what they were doing, but I was more interested in how they executed in daily operations on the ground where ministry culture gets lived out. They were generous to share budgets, management details, and operational ideas from board development to personnel evaluation. And through these years, we've kept those connections with Azusa strong. Jon Wallace, their current president, is a colleague I deeply admire, and I've borrowed more than a few of his ideas— maybe he's taken home some of mine as well.

Talking about a different culture is one thing, but it is very different to go touch it up close, and I know that our connection with Azusa was an accelerator in our organizational culture change, which has led to the tripling of our enrollment.

Step #10—Purposefully pause.

As discussed in chapter 10, a ministry can only accept so much change at one time—there are limits. With organizational cultural shifts this also is true, and maybe more so, because these changes go to the core of the comfort zone of people. Thus, it is helpful in this long-term process of shifting organizational culture to take periodic time out to slow the press of change. As a leader, you might be ready to push forward, but others may need a rest before they can absorb the next round of shifts.

Look for natural pauses that give opportunity for those working with you to catch their breath and internalize what has happened so far. On a college campus, those breaks are programmed into our calendar with sprints of activity in the fall and spring semesters, separated by a different pace for the summer, and a near dead stop over Christmas. Most ministries do not have these comfortable pauses, and thus effective leaders need to create them—and do so without fanfare to assure that the natural momentum continues while the pushing is backed off for a spell. This slowdown will bring about much more lasting organizational culture change in the long run.

Lasting Leadership

Pulling rabbits from a leader's hat always creates immediate value and applause. But genuine advance of a ministry comes about as purposeful ministry organizational culture change is carefully crafted over time. Not only is this the path to lasting success, but also, following this course will save many leaders the pain of running out of rabbits before their hat wears out, and like Rocky and Bullwinkle, they get abruptly pulled off the stage of leadership.

13

Catching the Wind of God

I am convinced one of the core problems of evangelical leaders is that too often we've stopped trying to catch the wind of God in our sails because we've become fairly effective at creating our own independent power to get God's work done. We can deploy plans, strategies, and best practices, but at the end of the day, we require a determined godly focus to make it far into the future with those we lead. And even though our motors can propel us forward to do many good things in ministry, we will miss catching the wind of God when our motors are revved rather than our sails mended.

There is a world of difference between powerboats and sailboats. And those differences are critical benchmarks for each of us in ministry leadership. I pray you might be willing to turn off the power of your organization's agenda and the best ideas that drive you—and instead consider the question, "Are you building a sailboat that will catch the wind of God, or are you only fine-tuning the engine on your powerboat so that you can keep going no matter which way the wind is blowing?" The powerboat framework is antithetical to the longview.

No Bible character lost more of his power, strength, and ability than Job. He was one who had the resources, faith, and insight to make almost anything happen. But he desired to always fill his sails with the wind of God—even when those winds blew him into a terrible storm. In his final explanation of his predicament, Job said, "God alone understands the way to wisdom; he knows where it can be found, for he looks throughout the whole earth and sees everything under the heavens" (Job 28:23–24).

If we are to catch the wind of God in our sails and go wherever those winds take us, we must begin with the unshakable understanding that God alone knows the way—knows the place where wisdom is found. Ultimately, the godly view is the view that aligns with God's will, revealed and unrevealed, for our organization. If we want the action plans coming out of our ministries to have significance, we must get out of our powerboats and step into boats whose sails are filled with the wind of God to take us to the place where wisdom is found.

In our ministry leadership we have a fundamental choice to make every day—and although the answer is easy, the implementation is difficult:

- Would we rather set out to achieve a set of sharply defined goals by revving up the engines to create the best programs, the best ministry concepts, and the best future our well-trained minds could imagine?

OR

- Would we rather go wherever the wind of God might take us?

While the second choice is clearly our desire, too often we live, plan, and work as if our direction is totally dependent on the power we can generate and the best course we can envision.

Sailboats versus Powerboats of Ministry

As the ways of the church have become influenced by our culture, too many Christian ministries have constructed powerboats that charge ahead, essentially ignoring the wind of God—at least until the wind becomes too strong, threatening to capsize them. Instead, God wants us to prepare to catch His wind by using our God-given gifts to build a sailboat that will go only where the Lord leads us.

Six contrasting benchmarks between powerboats and sailboats can help assure we catch the wind of God in the leadership of our ministry.

1. Are You Trusting the Wind?

With a sailboat, everything is designed to trust in the patterns of the wind; in contrast, a powerboat is constructed around trust in the motor. This fundamental question is the starting point in the shipyard. You have to choose one way or the other. The powerboat's performance may be slightly impacted by the wind, and the sailboat may have a small motor for special use—but primarily, you either are a sailor who trusts the wind, or one who trusts the motor.

Are we followers of Christ who are going to trust God or trust what power we can generate on His behalf? Are we satisfied with a powerboat that keeps us close to shore, or are we willing to build a

sailboat that can go as far as God desires? Are we clinging to a powerboat that is well tuned and running smoothly, or are we willing to
live in the risk and vulnerability of sailing where God leads us?

This is the core question Jesus asked His disciples as they sailed
together across the Sea of Galilee.

> *They got into a boat and started out. As they sailed across,
> Jesus settled down for a nap. But soon a fierce storm came
> down on the lake. The boat was filling with water, and
> they were in real danger.*
>
> *The disciples went and woke him up, shouting,
> "Master, Master, we're going to drown!"*
>
> *When Jesus woke up, he rebuked the wind and the
> raging waves. Suddenly the storm stopped and all was
> calm. Then he asked them, "Where is your faith?"*
>
> *The disciples were terrified and amazed. "Who
> is this man?" they asked each other. "When he gives a
> command, even the wind and waves obey him!" (Luke
> 8:22–25)*

Elizabethan Vice Admiral Sir Francis Drake desired to trust in
the wind of God rather than in his own power when he prayed:

> Disturb us, Lord, when we are too pleased with ourselves;
> when our dreams have come true because we dreamed too
> little; when we arrived safely because we sailed too close to
> the shore.

> Disturb us, Lord, when with the abundance of things we possess, we have lost our thirst for the waters of life.
>
> Disturb us, Lord, to dare more boldly; to venture on wider seas where storms will show Your mastery; where losing sight of land, we shall find the stars.[1]

As a leader seeking God's desires, will you look past the small body of water you know well and see the vastness of the sea? Will you choose not to be confined by self-generated power and trust the wind of God to discover the fullness He has for your ministry?

Christian researchers cite some overwhelming statistics that are not just numbers—they represent precious individuals and pressing ministry needs:

- There are 1 billion illiterate people in the world.
- There will be 50,000 new urban slum-dwellers today and every day.
- By the year 2025, 70 percent of all Christians will lack access to basic needs of food, water, shelter, and medical care.
- The number of abandoned and aborted children will double in twenty years to 280 million a year.
- There are 100 million people who call themselves Christian but are unaffiliated with any church.
- 70 percent of evangelicals know very little about the world's 1.8 billion unevangelized people.

- During the past twenty-five years, nine of ten new missionaries were sent out to already-reached people groups.
- The people groups most responsive to Christianity have consistently been shown to be the least-evangelized groups.[2]

When we see the challenge before us, we would give up right now if our trust were in only the power of our own motor. We are a small boat in a huge ocean, and we must trust the wind of God to fill our sails. Against the rough seas ahead, we do not have the power to take our boat where it needs to go.

Only if we trust the wind and know the wind will we sail on these waters of ministry to which God calls us. And *if* we trust the wind, we must be responsive to that wind rather than self-determining our direction. In a sailboat, we don't go wherever we want to go. Sailors only go where the wind allows them, and thus must work with the wind and within the laws that govern it, rather than setting an iron-grip course.

For most of us in leadership, that's scary. We don't want to put our trust in what we can't control—or even worse, what we may think is unpredictable. But the wind of God will not disappoint us. And we can be responsive to that wind when firmly grounded in our understanding of God's nature and God's unchanging ways.

2. Are You Focused Outward?

In a sailboat, we are looking at the water, listening to the wind and, most importantly, attending to the subtle ways the boat responds.

An experienced sailor sails as much by hearing as by seeing. In listening to the sails, the ropes, the water against the keel, and the creaks of the boat, a good sailor can almost see the wind and know how it is blowing. On the other hand, in a powerboat, you can't hear the wind, you can't hear the sea, and you can't hear the boat—all you hear is the motor. Or as one old sailor contrasted it, "A sailing vessel is alive in a way that no ship with mechanical power could ever be."

As leaders, we naturally look to our intellect, insights, experience, and ideas to guide these boats of ours. But our motor of ministry activity can sometimes get so loud that we can't begin to hear the wind, much less feel how our boat is responding to the wind.

Our ministry motors—the engines of aggressive programs, activities, and initiatives—can drown out our ability to hear the wind and know how the wind and boat are interacting. If our motor is cranked up to full speed, we get going so fast that the most vital and strategic ministry opportunities become a blur as we speed by them.

But if we focus on the sail and sky instead of the motor and power, we will be looking up and out, rather than staring down and in. The contrast couldn't be starker—and this is a critical benchmark to examine if we are catching the wind of God instead of powering our own motorboat. If we focus on our motor, we not only miss the wind of God, but we even forget that God gave us the gifts that allowed us to build that motor in the first place. So we doubly miss the blessings of God.

The Polish novelist and sailor Joseph Conrad wrote, "The true peace of God begins at any point 1,000 miles from the nearest land."

As a leader, have you ever been so far from land that you had to focus on the vastness of the sky because your motor wouldn't do you any good that far from your secure harbor? To catch the wind of God, our focus must be on the limitless power of Jesus instead of on the power of a motor that never allows us to stray from shore.

3. Are You Prepared?

While on vacation a few years ago I wanted to rent a little sailboat. This was a real act of giving from my wife, who doesn't swim but was willing to go along because I assured her I knew how to do it—even though I'd never been on a sailboat before. It looked simple as I watched others sail from shore, and the man renting the boats assured me that it was easy. So off we went on a calm afternoon to sail gently on the beautiful aqua water—until the wind shifted, the water got choppy, and a giant sea turtle nearly as big as our boat came to inspect.

The wind was pushing us out to sea, the turtle was following, and I had no idea how to get that boat turned around. I finally beached it on a little strip of land and waited for the wind to shift so that we could somehow get back to the dock—while my sailing partner graciously resisted a totally justified "I told you so."

If we are to catch the wind of God, we can't just jump in a sailboat and go like we can in a powerboat, because preparation of a sailboat requires extensive study, meticulous maintenance, and careful forethought, while a powerboat gives immediate gratification with little priming. As leaders, we must make constant preparation, not immediate activity, our highest priority. I'm convinced part of the reason leaders are drawn to motors rather than to catching the wind of God is that, somehow, it feels more productive.

If we can go, rather than prepare, isn't that more effective?

If we are pushing so hard we're out of breath, isn't that proof that what we do for God is important?

If we feel desperately needed by those around us, isn't that a sign our ministry is worthwhile?

The world may tell us that gas-and-go is more productive, but it will not prepare us to catch the wind of God. Sailing will take much preparation, and maintenance must be ingrained into every decision, every action, every day, or we will slip back to the immediate gratification of running on our own power.

Bill Pinkney, the first African-American to sail solo around the world is often quoted saying, "The sea is the only place where it doesn't matter if you are rich or poor, black or white. The only thing the sea cares about is whether you are prepared."[3] And proper preparation requires that we are constantly aware of how each part of the boat is intertwined with every other part—every sail, rope, plank, halyard, gunwale, rudder, tiller, cleat, beam, jib, batten, and the dozens of other parts of a sailing vessel are deeply dependent on each other if the wind of God is to be caught.

In the same way, in our ministries every part is the most important part, if we are to catch the wind of God. Every single person in your ministry is critical to God's plan. And while the public sees the leadership and spokespeople as the masts and sails of our ships, it is often the less visible parts that ensure we are prepared to catch the wind of God.

4. Are You Responding to the Wind?

There have been scores of books written about the romance of sailing around the world. But I can't find any books about those who drove their powerboat as far as it would go on a tank of gas. The powerboats we build may go fast—and those speeds may impress others. In contrast, God's wind usually gets us there much more slowly than we might desire, although it always gets us there just in time.

If there is one law of God's wind I've worked the most to build into my life, it is that God's timing is never wrong. And the patience to wait for the wind of God is sometimes especially frustrating when I would rather build a powerboat and get there soon. I've seen so many times in my own life and in the lives of others that human plans may create speed for a short time, but God's wind gives the boat limitless endurance. I thank the Lord I am growing in patience through the years, learning to wait for God's perfect timing.

But not only is the speed of a sailboat dramatically different—even the way it turns is different. Have you ever watched a large sailboat in operation? You don't just turn the wheel and change course. No, in response to how the wind shifts, the sailors anticipate when they are going to turn and then, with one well-orchestrated movement that has been practiced over and over, the boat changes course.

In contrast, the powerboats we drive abruptly maneuver back and forth, chasing after the latest new opportunity and tossing from side to side all those who are in the boat with us. Our direction must be grounded in the limitless endurance of the wind of

God, even when the speed frustrates us. And our patience must be built into the purposeful turns that God brings into our lives.

5. Are You Gentle?

I was fishing knee deep in calm water near the pass from a bay to the ocean in Alabama. It was a quiet, peaceful, and very relaxing place to be. But about three o'clock in the afternoon the first big fishing boat began to head back to shore. And everything changed. The boat was one hundred meters away, but as it went by it created huge waves that not only got me soaked, but also scared away all the fish. It was noisy, it reeked of diesel fuel, and there was no telling what it was putting into the water from the motor. It impacted everything in its path.

But the interesting thing about the disruption and pollution of a motorboat is that if you are on the boat, rather than near the boat, you don't even notice the havoc you've caused. You are long gone by the time your wake knocks all the other boats around.

And the same thing happens in ministry when relationships, programs, plans, competition, cultural insensitivity, or even the righteous arrogance of our egos and our logos become like motorboats—rough, self-centered, power based, and polluting. In fact, on a broad level, when we turn up the power of our ministry motors, our pollutants, noise, and disruption can created a dead zone that scares away all the fish and the other fishermen for a long time to come.

In contrast, have you ever been near the shore when a sailboat came by? Everyone wants to gaze upon it. The wake a sailboat leaves doesn't disrupt anything around it. It gives off no pollution of noise or fuel. And the beauty of its gentle nature makes you relax just to have it come close.

What would our ministry reports, our fund raising, and our accountability to each other be like if we were first required to look back to assure we have not created a powerful wake, strong pollution, or fishing dead zones before we were allowed to move forward with our next initiative?

6. Are You Genuine?

Sailing looks so relaxing, but nothing could be further from the truth. It is challenging, constant work that demands you stay attentive and use your best gifts. In contrast, a powerboat is fairly predictable, offering a relatively secure day on the water. The one that looks graceful and appealing demands hard work, and the one that goes fast and looks powerful demands little.

In our effort to be useful in God's service, we build powerboats to go running around making plans on God's behalf. But in doing so, we take the easy way out. I believe we build those powerboats because we are fearful that the sailboat that catches the wind of God does not really need us as leaders and will only call for us to lounge around on the deck and wait for the wind. And of course, we have it backward.

Catching the wind of God will press us into the greatest service we can imagine and will push us harder than we ever thought we could go. If we remain in our powerboat, life's journey will not go too far, but it will always be fairly comfortable.

In the powerboat we may put on the right kind of hat and be labeled a sailor, but the sailboat demands that we be genuine sailors. If we want to catch the wind of God, we must be the real thing. You can't just put up a sail in the middle of a powerboat and expect that it will become a sailboat. Leaders must abandon their powerboats and move into a totally different kind of craft.

Sometimes sailing on the wind of God is hanging on for dear life, and sometimes it is waiting patiently while no wind blows. But no matter the circumstances, our task is to have our boats and our sails prepared to catch the wind of God—however it may blow.

The One, Great Wind

Every summer and early fall, gentle winds begin to gather along the Tropic of Cancer in West Africa. They seem to circulate without purpose or direction until they move offshore and start to pull up warm water, and the humidity of the season enables those winds to gain speed and circulation. Periodically, about a week later, they cross the entire Atlantic Ocean and are usually kissing the northern edge of South America when they attract other winds and strengthen into what becomes a named tropical storm, which can eventually become a hurricane. Katrina did just that in 2005 and devastated my campus in Jackson, 150 miles inland, although we were among the more fortunate ones in the path of the storm.

But being so personally involved with this hurricane gave me four fresh understandings of the wind and how the physical wind often mirrors the wind of God.

The wind is interconnected around the world in ways that we don't understand or often see. I can feel what blows in Mississippi, but that wind is pulled together from Africa, South America, the Caribbean, Central America, and who knows where else. All the motions of wind around the world are interlinked in complex ways to create what I experience. And although I can't see it or always understand why, I need to know that the physical wind I feel is part of a globally connected movement—the same as the spiritual wind of God.

A strong wind doesn't start at full speed, but it always begins with only a slight breeze. And we see time and time again that this is how God likes to work: seeds that become huge trees, little children who become strong leaders, and seemingly small ministries with monumental eternal significance. Knowing the nature of how strong winds build, the best sailors are attentive to the slightest change in the wind, for it is a signal of what is to come—as we should be too, if we want to catch the wind of God.

The wind is a visual demonstration of the power of God, which can topple any structure, break down the best defenses, and uproot that which we assume has been deeply planted.

The most powerful wind also demonstrates God's control. At the height of the hurricane I saw the winds go from 140 miles per hour to 10 miles per hour in a few seconds as the eye passed over the coast of Mississippi—and then back to that enormous force a half hour later. And it brought a new reality to the understanding that even when the winds are so strong that we feel overwhelmed and helpless, God still controls the wind. The eye of a hurricane is like God's signature—reminding us that even in the midst of the worst He can still create calm.

The wind of God is always present, most often as a guiding, gentle breeze. But there will be times when we don't feel that wind at all, and in rare times it will blow so hard we'll feel helpless. Remember there will always be purpose, order, and intentionality to the wind of God.

May we as leaders live, work, and relate to each other in such a way that we too would understand that the most impressive ministry motors we might develop fade in comparison to the boat whose sails are filled with God's wind. While we may feel proud when powerboats of ministry are big, well built, and polished, even a small, poorly crafted, and worn sailboat will outdistance a powerboat every time—because only the sailboat is able to catch the wind of God.

Notes

Introduction

1. Mark Gottfredson, Steve Schaubert, and Hernan Saenz, "The New Leader's Guide to Diagnosing the Business," *Harvard Business Review* 86.2 (February 2008): 62–73.

Chapter 1

1. Leonard M. Lodish and Carl F. Mela, "If Brands Are Built over Years, Why Are They Managed over Quarters?" *Harvard Business Review* 85.7/8 (July/August 2007): 104–112.

Chapter 2

1. Jim Collins, "Level 5 Leadership: The Triumph of Humility and Fierce Resolve," *Harvard Business Review* 79.1 (January 2001): 66–76.

2. Roderick M. Kramer, "The Harder They Fall," *Harvard Business Review* 81.10 (2003): 58–66.

3. John Stott, "Pride, Humility, and God," in *Alive to God*, ed. J. I. Packer and Loren Wilkinson (Vancouver, BC,: Regent College Publishing, 1992), 111.

4. Rick Warren, interview by Larry King, *Larry King Live*, CNN, November 22, 2004.

Chapter 3

1. Amy Schurr, "Qualities of Good Leaders and Employees," NetworkWorld, November 6, 2003, http://www.networkworld.com/newsletters/itlead/2003/1103itlead2.html.

2. "When the Boss Is a Jerk," *The Week*, November 11, 2005, www.theweek.com.

3. Holly J. Morris, "Happiness Explained," *U.S. News & World Report*, September 3, 2001, 46–54.

253

Chapter 4

1. J. I. Packer, *Rediscovering Holiness* (Ann Arbor, MI: Servant Publications, 1992), 121.

2. Collins, "Level 5 Leadership," 104–112.

3. Ibid.

4. T. O. Jacobs, *Leadership and Exchange in Formal Organizations* (Alexandria, VA: HumRRO, 1970).

5. Daniel Goleman, *Emotional Intelligence: Why It Can Matter More Than IQ* (New York: Bantam, 1995), 54.

6. Elton Trueblood, *Quarterly Yoke Letter* 36.2 (June 1994): 2.

7. C. S. Lewis, *Mere Christianity* (New York: HarperCollins, 2001), 134.

Chapter 5

1. Ruth Graham, "A Hearing Heart," *Decision,* January 1970, 12.

Chapter 6

1. Archibald D. Hart, "Being Moral Isn't Always Enough," *Leadership* 9.2 (1988): 24–31.

2. Richard John Neuhaus, *Death on a Friday Afternoon* (New York: Basic Books, 2001), 9.

Chapter 9

1. These illustrations were shared in a December 1998 small-group conversation in Omaha, Nebraska, led by Dr. Don Clifton, then-chairman of The Gallup Organization.

Chapter 12

1. Debra Lea Thorsen, "Optimizing Your Company for the 21st Century," *Culture Builders,* www.culturebuilders.com.

2. John Hamm, "The Five Messages Leaders Must Manage," *Harvard Business Review* 84.5 (May 2006): 114–123.

3. Hirotaka Takeuchi, Emi Osono, and Norihiko Shimizu, "The Contradictions That Drive Toyota's Success," *Harvard Business Review* 86.6 (June 2008): 96–104.

Chapter 13
1. Sir Francis Drake, public domain.
2. Todd M. Johnson, Peter F. Crossing, and Bobby Jangsun Ryu, "Looking Forward: An Overview of World Evangelization, 2005–2025," (special report for the Lausanne 2004 Forum on World Evangelization, Center for the Study of Global Christianity, Pattaya, Thailand, 2004).
3. Bill Pinkney (speech, Black Boater's Summit, 2000).